# UN
# BR
# EA
# KA
# BLE

# UNBREAKABLE

A Changemaker's Guide

Lois Castillo

ARCHWAY
PUBLISHING

Copyright © 2025 Lois Castillo.

All rights reserved. No part of this book may be used or reproduced by any means, graphic, electronic, or mechanical, including photocopying, recording, taping or by any information storage retrieval system without the written permission of the author except in the case of brief quotations embodied in critical articles and reviews.

This book is a work of non-fiction. Unless otherwise noted, the author and the publisher make no explicit guarantees as to the accuracy of the information contained in this book and in some cases, names of people and places have been altered to protect their privacy.

Archway Publishing books may be ordered through booksellers or by contacting:

Archway Publishing
1663 Liberty Drive
Bloomington, IN 47403
www.archwaypublishing.com
844-669-3957

Because of the dynamic nature of the Internet, any web addresses or links contained in this book may have changed since publication and may no longer be valid. The views expressed in this work are solely those of the author and do not necessarily reflect the views of the publisher, and the publisher hereby disclaims any responsibility for them.

Any people depicted in stock imagery provided by Getty Images are models, and such images are being used for illustrative purposes only. Certain stock imagery © Getty Images.

ISBN: 978-1-6657-7850-3 (sc)
ISBN: 978-1-6657-7852-7 (hc)
ISBN: 978-1-6657-7851-0 (e)

Library of Congress Control Number: 2025910841

Print information available on the last page.

Archway Publishing rev. date: 7/30/2025

**For Ramon, Ramon III, and Xavier —**
My heart, my home, my greatest why.
Thank you for giving me the space, the grace,
and the quiet strength to write this into being.
Your love is the unshakable foundation beneath every word.

To all the DEI practitioners, cultural architects, and other changemakers:
You are the quiet disruptors, the storytellers, and the bridge-builders who weave justice and hope into every space you enter. This is for your resilience, your radical love, and your belief that even the smallest shifts can spark revolutions.

May you always know you are seen, valued, and *unbreakable*.

*Luis Castillo*
*2025*

# CONTENTS

Foreword ................................................................................ ix
Introduction .......................................................................... xi

Chapter 1    Self-Care ............................................................ 1
Chapter 2    Developing Your Self-Care Plan ..................... 13
Chapter 3    Mental and Emotional Health ...................... 27
Chapter 4    Physical Well-Being ....................................... 33
Chapter 5    Inspiring Stories of Self-Care Success ........... 41
Chapter 6    Personal Development and Growth ............. 47
Chapter 7    Cultivating Emotional Intelligence ............... 59
Chapter 8    Building Resilience ........................................ 65
Chapter 9    Psychological Safety ...................................... 73
Chapter 10   Physical Safety ............................................... 83
Chapter 11   Stories of Safety and Inclusivity .................... 91
Chapter 12   Conflict Resolution and Resilience ............. 103
Chapter 13   Leading with Inclusive Excellence .............. 109
Chapter 14   Allies and Advocacy ..................................... 113
Chapter 15   Core Values .................................................. 123
Chapter 16   Core Values In Action ................................. 133
Chapter 17   Measures of Success .................................... 143
Chapter 18   The Everlasting Journey of Growth and Purpose ........ 147

Bonus Chapter—When You've Had Enough: Creating
Your Exit Strategy .............................................................. 151
Appendix A—Resources That Shaped My Journey ......... 159

# FOREWORD

The toolkit Lois has laid out in this book is not a collection of strategies; it is a lifeline cast into the often rocky sea of DEI work and practitioners, offering support and perspective; and when you don't see a blueprint, sometimes you have to build and then *be* the blueprint.

This is a reality for many diversity, equity, and inclusion leaders and practitioners—individuals who have, in many cases, pursued, shifted into, and evolved their careers intentionally to support this important work while being among the first, only, or few in their workspaces to take up the title and the weight of the responsibility that comes with the role.

Beyond that, those who have pursued the work with the intent to focus on purpose, drive impact, and systemic change are often met with the realization that these ambitions within themselves, juxtaposed with the realities of complex and often DEI-immature corporate settings, compel them to take on new skills, armor, and postures to advance even a *fraction* of their work.

Meanwhile, many are often underestimated, under-resourced, and disempowered relative to their peers in other practices, departments, and teams advancing business objectives in the same systems.

At the same time, the work itself is being challenged and questioned, and individuals are caught in the crosshairs of their practice being critiqued, narrowing in on their own capabilities and personhood being challenged.

If this resonates with you or anyone in your orbit, this book is for you.

In my journey through multiple DEI leadership roles, I regularly wished for a guide, sage wisdom, or tested considerations that would not only support me in doing my work to a degree of satisfaction and impact but also allow me to take care of and sustain myself in the process, even solace to those who need it now more than ever.

The road of a DEI practitioner is one paved with challenges that are unique in their scope and emotional toll. It demands not only a sharp intellect and unwavering dedication but also a heart resilient enough to withstand and rise above systemic resistance. It requires *years* of intention and a commitment to sustainable transformation over superficial fixes—a commitment that Lois understands and brilliantly encapsulates in her writing.

This book is a resource and salve for anyone who has ambitions to continue to pursue or take on this essential work in spaces still grappling with his or her own evolution. It equips practitioners not just with the tools needed for the day-to-day nuances of DEI work but with the wisdom to navigate the things that are quietly shared but loudly felt by so many.

I have lived the life that this book seeks to address and ease. The seasoned insights and actionable knowledge outlined in this book would have been a treasure during my tenure as a DEI leader.

Yet the beauty of this toolkit lies in its timeless relevance—crafted from lived experiences and shared truths—it offers each of us the chance to learn, grow, and, perhaps most importantly, to feel understood and less alone.

This is for the practitioners—the individuals who maintain the energy, intention, and audacity to do this work despite all barriers and friction.

As you take time out to tend to yourself and read this book, may you find in your words the strength, resolve, and necessary resilience to carry on this important work.

—Ronnie Dickerson Stewart, executive coach and leadership professional

# INTRODUCTION

Dear fellow practitioner,

Welcome to *Unbreakable*, a resource to help you along a journey that's as real and as human as it gets. As you dive into these pages, I want you to know that we're in this together. This book is more than just a collection of words—it's a piece of my heart, forged from my unwavering commitment to the often capricious world of diversity, equity, and inclusion (DEI).

What you're about to read is a result of countless moments of learning, engaging, and, yes, sometimes even unlearning. It's all part of the path we walk as practitioners. In sharing my experiences, my aim is not just to pass on knowledge but also to offer you a sanctuary—a place to pause, reflect, and find comfort in knowing that you're never alone on this journey.

In these pages, you'll discover practical tools tailored just for you. They're not here to add to your hustle, but rather to give you a moment to catch your breath and equip yourself with strategies you can put into action in your daily work. Think of this book as more than just reading material; it's your partner in our collective mission to make the world a more inclusive and fairer place.

You see, even though our work can sometimes make us feel like lone wolves, this book stands as proof that we're a bonded community, united in our collective actions. We're a mosaic of individuals, each thread crucial, each story significant. I hope that as you engage with these pages, you feel that sense of camaraderie and support. Remember, your efforts, your struggles, and your triumphs are not only yours, they're shared, understood, and valued.

So thank you for joining me on this adventure. May this book be a guiding light, a reminder of the impact of your work, and a testament to the strength that comes from our combined efforts.

Warmest regards,
Lois

PS: Throughout this book I suggest tools and strategies that have supported me on my journey. Please remember that I am a certified coach, not a medical professional. However, based on my lived experiences, I highly recommend everyone have a qualified therapist on their personal "board of trustees."

\*

Fellow practitioners, welcome!

This guidebook is designed to empower you with the skills necessary to practice self-reflection and sustainable self-care, ensure your mental and physical safety, pursue personal development, and establish the nonnegotiable core values that are key to guiding us through our meaningful but often arduous work. Welcome to a resource crafted with personal insights gained from our shared journey as professionals who are unbreakable in our mission to make an inclusive world a reality for all.

Having walked this path myself, I extend a warm and compassionate welcome to you. This toolkit serves as a beacon of guidance in recognition of the immense importance and the formidable challenges we encounter within the realm of diversity, equity, and inclusion. Our role is nothing short of transformational. We are the architects of change, weaving threads of diversity into the very fabric of our organizations. We stand as advocates for those whose voices may not otherwise be heard, and we shine a light on systemic inequalities that must be addressed.

But let's be honest; our work is not for the fainthearted. It's not just about diversity training or policy adjustments. It's about shifting cultures, dismantling deep-rooted biases, and navigating complex, often uncomfortable conversations. It's about finding common ground where divisions run deep. It's about maintaining resilience in the face of resistance.

In the midst of this challenging terrain, our core values become our North Star. They are the bedrock upon which we build our strategies, initiatives, and responses to adversity. This toolkit emphasizes the significance of nonnegotiable core values, beliefs and actions that are unwavering and uncompromising in their commitment to fairness, inclusivity, and justice. Our values serve as our guiding principles, moral compass, and source of strength. They are the assurance that, even in the face of adversity, we remain resolute in our dedication to creating a more equitable world.

I want you to know that you're not alone in this journey. As practitioners, we will face pushback and skepticism that lead to exhaustion at times, but we are united by a shared purpose. This work, though challenging, is deeply rewarding. It's about impacting lives, fostering belonging, and creating workplaces where everyone can thrive.

This toolkit is a reflection of our collective commitment to realizing those outcomes. Together, we can continue making strides toward a more inclusive and equitable future, knowing that our journey is not solitary, but one we share with countless others who stand for DEI principles. Thank you for your dedication to this important mission.

**Note to Readers**

This book is for those driving change—DEI practitioners, ERG leaders, cultural changemakers, talent professionals, activists, and those working within public, private, educational, for-profit, and nonprofit spaces. Throughout these pages, I will refer to you as *practitioners,* because this work is more than a role; it's a commitment to building a more just and inclusive world. This journey is yours, and this book is here to support you every step of the way.

# CHAPTER 01

## Self-Care

*Self-care means giving the world the best of you, instead of what's left of you.*

**KATIE REED**

Hey,

I want to begin this chapter with a sense of vulnerability and honesty, because self-care is a topic that has touched my heart deeply. As we dive in, I want you to understand why this subject matters to me on a profound level.

Our work in the realm of diversity, equity, and inclusion (DEI) is a labor of love, with each one of us deeply committed to making the world a better place. However, this dedication, while incredibly noble, can sometimes lead us down a perilous path—one on which we begin to neglect the most important people in this journey: ourselves.

I found myself in that very place not too long ago. As I poured my heart and soul into this work, I noticed the toll it was taking on my own well-being. The long hours, the sleepless nights, the missed doctors' appointments, and the lack of healthy boundaries began to leave their mark. In convincing myself that I needed to be there for everyone else all the time, I neglected my own physical and mental health. I forgot about the person who needed me most—myself. I failed to take care of my body or process the emotional weight of the harm we're fighting against: to digest the complex feelings that arise when we confront the injustices of the world.

My experience taught me a vital lesson: self-care is not a luxury; it's an absolute necessity. When we neglect ourselves, we also undermine our capacity to make a real difference. We can't be effective champions for change if we're physically, emotionally, and mentally running on empty.

In this chapter, we will explore the importance of self-care in the context of our work. We will delve into what self-care means for practitioners, understanding its impact on both our personal well-being and the very effectiveness of our efforts. Self-care is not selfish. It's a fundamental right, a critical means of self-preservation and a crucial aspect of sustaining our commitment to this work. It's an act of self-compassion and resilience, a way to build the strength needed to navigate the intersectionality of the harms we confront daily.

So as we explore the pages of this chapter, remember that you are not alone on your journey. We all share in the experiences and challenges that come with this work. Let's embrace self-care as a collective practice and honor ourselves as we honor the pursuit of a more inclusive world.

In solidarity,
Lois

## THE IMPORTANCE OF SELF-CARE

In the whirlwind of our work, it's easy to get caught up in the demands and responsibilities that come with advocating for diversity, equity, and inclusion. However, we soon learn it is paramount to recognize that prioritizing self-care is not an indulgence; it is an absolute necessity.

True self-care goes beyond the conventional notions of relaxation and pampering. It encompasses maintaining intentional and holistic practices that sustain our physical, emotional, mental, and spiritual well-being, which in turn allows us to be effective advocates for change. The most difficult part of holistic wellness is finding balance in all these areas of our lives, but it is crucial to effectively supporting ourselves and the work.

Following are four key aspects of holistic self-care practices for practitioners:

### 1. Cultivating Emotional Resilience

- **Mindfulness and meditation:** Our work often involves navigating emotionally charged conversations and addressing systemic injustices. Practicing mindfulness and meditation can help us stay grounded, manage stress, and build emotional resilience.
- **Therapy and counseling:** Regular therapy or counseling sessions can provide a safe space for practitioners to process their own experiences, challenges, and emotions related to their work. It can also help prevent burnout and compassion fatigue. For most of my career, I have seen a therapist who has kept me grounded and helped me navigate some of my most challenging times doing this work. I'm currently in the process of looking for a new therapist, and that may be one reason why I'm now writing this book. A lot like journaling, it's given me a place to process the stress and difficult emotions that come with this work. But I trust and believe I will not go through 2025 without professional support.

## 2. Maintaining Physical Health

- **Regular exercise:** Engaging in regular physical activity supports both physical health and mental well-being. Make time for activities you enjoy, whether it's yoga, running, dancing, or any other form of exercise. Hell, do this shit even if you *don't* enjoy it. Become disciplined and consistent with your physical health. This isn't negotiable; you must maintain physical health to thrive as a practitioner.
- **Balanced nutrition:** A well-balanced diet is essential for sustained energy and mental clarity. Prioritizing nutritious meals and staying hydrated can contribute to overall well-being. Truthfully, this section is short because I am still learning to become disciplined about my own health in a positive way. So know that I am writing these words to hold myself accountable as much as I am writing them for you.

## 3. Building a Supportive Community

- **Networking and peer support:** Remember you are not the only practitioner out there, and we can benefit immensely from connecting with peers in our field or similar roles. Sharing experiences, strategies, and challenges with others who understand the unique demands of DEI work can be invaluable.
- **Your personal board of trustees:** Be deliberate about building this trusted support group. These are the people in your life who will offer diverse perspectives, assist in advancing your career, provide friendship, ensure accountability, extend emotional support, and offer guidance for conflict resolution. By actively engaging with and leveraging the collective wisdom and support of your board of trustees, you can effectively navigate the complexities of this work, continuously develop as a professional, and maximize your impact in promoting diversity, equity, and inclusion. Note: These trusted advisors don't all have to be in our field or do the

same work we do. Many of my trustees are not even in my industry, but they are my champions who never fail to support me.

## 4. Embracing Boundaries

Setting and maintaining healthy boundaries is not just a professional necessity; it's a form of self-respect and a means to protect our energy and prevent burnout. Boundaries allow us to ensure a balanced approach to our work, and it all comes down to saying no with grace. This is not just an act of self-preservation; it's a vital strategy for sustainability in our personal and professional lives. Embracing the power of a graceful no can be transformative, allowing us to maintain our energy, focus, and commitment to what truly matters.

But I would be remiss without acknowledging that for many people, saying no comes with a sense of guilt. Moving past that guilt starts with understanding that saying no is not just acceptable but necessary. It's a boundary you set for others as well as for yourself—a declaration of your values, priorities, and limits. To ease the discomfort that often accompanies saying no, consider these five steps:

- **Acknowledge your feelings:** Recognize and accept that feeling guilty about saying no is normal. But also understand that guilt does not signify wrongdoing. It's often a reflection of our desire to help and please others, a common trait in those dedicated to service and support.
- **Reflect on your priorities:** Each time you're faced with a request, take a moment to consider how it aligns with your priorities and values. If it doesn't support your goals or well-being, it's OK to decline. Prioritizing doesn't make you selfish; it makes you focused and effective.
- **Practice self-compassion:** Be kind to yourself. Saying no can feel tough, but it's a necessary part of self-care. Remember, you cannot pour from an empty cup. By saying no to others, you are saying yes to yourself and your needs.

- **Communicate clearly and respectfully:** When you decide to say no, communicate your decision clearly and with respect. You don't owe extensive explanations or apologies. Remember, "no" is a complete sentence. But if that feels too harsh, a simple, "I'm sorry; I can't commit to this right now," is often enough.
- **Reframe your perspective:** Instead of viewing a no as a missed opportunity or a letdown, reframe it as an act of empowerment—for yourself and the person making the request. By being honest about your capacity, you are setting necessary boundaries, which ultimately lead to healthier expectations, interactions, and relationships.

Embracing the power of saying no with grace is an ongoing process. It requires practice, patience, and self-reflection. As you grow more comfortable with it, you'll find that it not only brings sustainability to your life but also enhances your ability to make meaningful contributions to the things that truly matter.

It's important to note that holistic self-care is a personalized journey, and what works best may differ greatly from one person to another. The key is to regularly assess your needs and make self-care practices a priority. Put them on your calendar as you would any other important event.

## DESIGNING WORK-LIFE BOUNDARIES

One of the most significant challenges we face doing this work is blurring the lines between our work and our personal lives. We've all heard plenty about *work-life* boundaries, but I feel it's smarter to put our lives first. Defining and establishing *life-work* boundaries is crucial for maintaining a healthy balance, especially for those in demanding roles such as ours.

Here are three steps to help establish these boundaries:

1. **Designate and respect your spaces:** Identify and set up a specific area in your home exclusively for work. This could be a home office, a particular table, or even a corner of a room that is

work-conducive. Next, create a separate space for relaxation that is free from work-related materials and distractions. This could be a comfortable chair, a reading nook, or a spot with a pleasant view. Respect the purpose of these spaces. When you're in your workspace, focus on work. When you're in your relaxation space, commit to leaving work behind.
2. **Establish clear time boundaries:** Establish a cutoff time each day when you consciously disconnect from work-related communication and activities. After this time you will not check emails, take calls, or perform any work-related tasks. Communicate these boundaries to colleagues, clients, and family members so they understand your availability and respect your off-hours. Use tools such as out-of-office replies or notification settings on your devices to reinforce these time boundaries when you are not working.
3. **Normalize and advocate for boundaries:** Understand that setting boundaries is an act of self-care and is vital for your well-being and the sustainability of your passion and your work. Regularly review and adjust your boundaries as needed. Life and work demands can change, and your boundaries should be flexible enough to accommodate these changes.

Encourage a culture of respect for personal boundaries within your workplace. Share strategies with colleagues and promote an environment in which everyone feels empowered to set the boundaries they need for balance.

By following these steps, you can create a structure that helps delineate your professional and personal lives. This structure not only supports your well-being but also enhances your effectiveness and longevity in your role. Remember, establishing boundaries is not a one-off task but a continuous process that requires commitment and adaptation.

Strong boundaries are not a sign of weakness or disengagement; they're a sign of self-care and self-preservation. They enable us to sustain our passion and dedication to the work in the long term, ensuring we can continue making a meaningful impact. So let's embrace boundaries as allies on our journey toward a healthier and more effective practice.

## THE IMPACT OF SELF-CARE

Why should practitioners make self-care a priority? The answer lies in the profound impact it has—not only on our personal lives but on our effectiveness as advocates for diversity, equity, and inclusion.

In this section, we explore three ways in which self-care positively influences our work:

### 1. Enhanced resilience

Self-care equips us with the resilience needed to face challenges and adversity head-on. Resilience is needed not only to endure challenges but also to thrive and make a lasting impact in our roles. Let's discuss how practicing self-care empowers us in three key areas of resilience to help us stay steadfast in our commitment to effecting change.

- **Emotional resilience:** Self-care fosters emotional resilience, which allows us to navigate emotionally charged situations effectively. For instance, emotional resilience built via grounding techniques like deep breathing has helped me confront resistance or hostility in DEI workshops or conversations. Emotional resilience allows you to respond calmly and empathetically, even in challenging circumstances, thus promoting a constructive dialogue.
- **Cognitive resilience:** This type of resilience allows practitioners to maintain mental clarity and sharpness when navigating complex organizations. Prioritizing self-care by dedicating time for adequate sleep, mindfulness meditation, or regular breaks helps us clear our minds, allowing us to think critically and make

well-informed decisions amid difficult and sometimes chaotic challenges.
- **Interpersonal resilience:** Self-care contributes to interpersonal resilience by enabling us to build and sustain positive relationships. In this work, we often interact with diverse groups, each with unique perspectives. By practicing self-care, we can better manage our own emotions, actively listen, and engage in empathetic communication. This fosters trust and collaboration, enhancing our ability to navigate initiatives effectively and maintain productive relationships with stakeholders.

## 2. Improved Emotional Intelligence

Nurturing our emotional well-being enhances our capacity for empathy, compassion, and effective communication, which I believe are foundational. Here are three key components to growing your emotional intelligence.

- **Self-awareness and reflection:** It's important for us to engage in regular self-awareness and reflection exercises to better understand our own emotions, biases, and triggers. For example, a friend, who has been doing this work for many years, keeps a journal about reactions to challenges and participates in mindfulness practices to stay attuned to emotional states. This self-awareness has helped them respond empathetically and compassionately to others' experiences and perspectives.
- **Empathy building:** We all must actively work on developing our empathy skills. One way to do that is by focusing on our own emotional well-being. Reading books or attending workshops that promote empathy and understanding of different perspectives helps nurture our own emotional intelligence. This helps us better connect people from diverse backgrounds, listen more attentively to their experiences, and build stronger relationships based on trust and mutual respect.

- **Conflict resolution and communication:** Effective communication skills can help us manage conflicts and facilitate difficult conversations. Taking care of our emotional well-being helps us remain composed during high-stress situations, actively listen to others' concerns, and express ourselves with empathy and clarity. This enables us to navigate disagreements and promote inclusivity more effectively within organizations or communities.

## 3. Role modeling

Whether you know it or not, you automatically became a role model when you signed up for this job. That means you play a pivotal role in setting examples within your organizations. Your actions and behaviors serve as a template for others to follow. One crucial aspect of being an effective role model is prioritizing self-care. Here's an in-depth explanation of what it means to be a role model by emphasizing self-care and its broader implications:

- **Leading by example:** By actively prioritizing self-care in our own lives, we demonstrate the importance of well-being and mental health to our colleagues and peers. So leave on time whenever you can. Don't work while sick. And take your vacation time. Bonus points for not monitoring email while you're off.
- **Fostering a culture of well-being:** Our commitment to self-care has a ripple effect within our organizations. When we openly embrace self-care practices, we contribute to fostering a culture of well-being. This culture extends beyond us and encourages others to take their well-being seriously as well. Employees and colleagues observe our actions and recognize that their organization values their health and happiness.
- **Promoting inclusivity:** Self-care is not a one-size-fits-all concept; it's about individualized well-being. By emphasizing self-care, we acknowledge the diversity of needs and experiences within our organization. This acknowledgment aligns with the

very principles we're working to instill. When others see us embracing self-care, it reinforces the truth that everyone's unique well-being needs are valid and worthy of attention.
- **Supporting sustainable impact:** By being role models for self-care, we contribute to the sustainability of our efforts and help to prevent the burnout and fatigue that are otherwise inevitable. Taking care of ourselves helps ensure that we have the energy, resilience, and enthusiasm to drive lasting change within our organizations.

In this chapter, we laid the groundwork for our journey through this practitioners' toolkit. We recognize that self-care isn't a one-size-fits-all solution; it's a personal journey that involves continuous self-reflection and adaptation. My aspiration is that, as you grasp the significance of self-care and its profound influence, you'll be motivated to integrate it seamlessly into your practice. The terms I've introduced in this chapter will reappear throughout this book. As you progress, we'll delve deeper, encouraging you to reflect and explore further.

# CHAPTER 02
## Developing Your Self-Care Plan

*Dear practitioners,*

*As you embark on the journey of developing your self-care plan, you'll notice that this chapter takes on a unique format—it's presented as a reflection journal. Why? Because I firmly believe that the path to effective self-care is paved with self-reflection.*

*In my own quest to create real change within myself and in the world, I've come to understand that self-care isn't just about pampering ourselves occasionally. It's about becoming intentional and disciplined in how we care for ourselves—physically, mentally, and emotionally. It's about making a commitment not only to the cause we champion but also to our own well-being. We need to lift ourselves up just as we do others.*

*I've learned that to be truly effective in our work, we must first be effective at self-care. I've realized that in this journey is a personal agreement we make with ourselves—a commitment to become disciplined about positive self-care practices.*

*This reflection journal serves as a space for you to document your thoughts, insights, and aspirations as you navigate the process of self-care planning. It is designed to encourage you to pause and consider your unique needs and goals. It will empower you to set intentions, create sustainable routines, and establish boundaries that safeguard your well-being and peace.*

*As you engage with this journal, remember that it's not just a collection of pages; it's a canvas for your growth. It's a tool to help you develop a self-care plan that is as unique as you are. It's a reminder that self-care is not selfish—it's an essential investment in yourself and your ability to drive meaningful change.*

*So embrace this chapter as your personal journey toward holistic well-being. Allow it to guide you in becoming intentional and disciplined about your self-care. And as you do, remember that taking care of yourself is not only an act of self-love but also a powerful act of sustainability and resilience in your practice.*

*In reflection and commitment,*
*Lois*

Before we embark on the journey of crafting your self-care plan, I'd like to share that a dear friend and sister in change often reminds me that it's imperative to pause and ground myself. This line of work is undoubtedly challenging and requires unwavering commitment. As we navigate the intricate intersectionality of our identities and strive to bring about cultural shifts in these transformative times, it's essential to remember why we have chosen this path. I turn to three fundamental questions that serve as my North Star, revisiting them twice a year to maintain clarity and accountability in my work.

## WHAT IS MY WHY?

The first question, "What is my Why?," dives deep into the core of my purpose. It reminds me of the driving force behind my dedication to DEI. Why have I chosen this line of work, and what propels me to continue this challenging path? Reflecting on my why keeps me rooted in my mission. It rekindles the passion that fuels my commitment to making a meaningful difference.

## WHAT DOES DEI MEAN TO ME?

The second question, "What does DEI mean to me?," prompts me to define my personal interpretation of diversity, equity, and inclusion. It's a dynamic and evolving field, and understanding its significance to me is crucial. This question helps me stay authentic as a practitioner, ensuring that my actions align with my values and beliefs. It guides me in nurturing a self-care plan that resonates with my unique vision of promoting inclusivity and equity.

## WHAT IS MY IMPACT?

The third question, "What is my impact?," encourages me to envision the lasting change I aspire to create in this field. It reminds me that my journey is not just about accomplishing tasks and projects; it's about leaving a meaningful legacy. Reflecting on this question clarifies within me the changes I aim to make. It underscores the importance of self-care as a means to sustain my well-being and resilience in pursuit of my goals.

I revisit these three questions twice a year—once at the beginning of the year, as I prepare for the challenges and opportunities ahead, and again at the end of the year, when I reflect on my accomplishments and hold myself accountable for the work I have done. This foundational introspection is critical for the effectiveness and discipline required in the world of DEI. It reminds me that self-care is not an indulgence but a necessity that enables me to be a more impactful advocate for a more inclusive and equitable world.

Now I invite you to pause and embrace the power of these three questions before embarking on your journey ahead. It's essential that you fully grasp and then anchor yourself in the profound purpose of your work. Before you craft your self-care plan, take this moment to connect with your inner drive and purpose. This introspection is the cornerstone of your journey, guiding you toward greater clarity, resilience, and intentionality in your pursuit of excellence in the DEI realm.

## YOUR TURN

What is your why?

_____

_____

_____

What does DEI mean to you?

_____

_____

_____

What is your impact?

_____

_____

_____

Now let's identify your emotional response. After reflecting on your why, your personal interpretation of DEI, and the impact you wish to have, describe in one or two words how you feel right now. Is it *empowered, challenged, motivated,* or something else? Briefly, what does this emotion reveal to you about your connection to the work?

_____

_____

Next, let's focus on your personal discovery. Reflecting on the answers to the three pivotal questions above, in one or two words, how do you feel about your journey ahead? Feelings could range from *hopeful* to *daunted*. What have you learned about your strengths, challenges, and the depth of your commitment to DEI through this process?

_____

_____

Now let's get into the meat and potatoes: our self-care plans.

## SELF-ASSESSMENT OF PERSONAL NEEDS

Before embarking on your self-care journey, it's crucial to assess your current well-being. This self-assessment can help you identify areas that may require attention and sets the foundation for a personalized self-care plan.

Rate each of the following statements on a scale of 1 to 5, with 1 being "strongly disagree" and 5 being "strongly agree."

1. **I prioritize self-care and make time for it regularly.**
    1
    2
    3
    4
    5

2. **I am satisfied with my work-life balance.**
    1
    2
    3
    4
    5

3. **I feel emotionally resilient and can effectively manage stress.**
    1
    2
    3
    4
    5

4. **I get enough quality sleep on a regular basis.**
    1
    2
    3
    4
    5

5. **I maintain a healthy and balanced diet.**
    1
    2
    3

    4
    5

6. **I engage in regular physical activity that I enjoy.**
    1
    2
    3
    4
    5

7. **I have a strong support system of family and friends.**
    1
    2
    3
    4
    5

8. **I am satisfied with my personal and professional relationships.**
    1
    2
    3
    4
    5

9. **I practice regular mindfulness or relaxation techniques.**
    1
    2
    3
    4
    5

10. **I have a sense of purpose and meaning in my life.**
    1
    2
    3

    4
    5

11. I am able to effectively manage my time and commitments.
    1
    2
    3
    4
    5

12. I feel financially secure and comfortable with my financial situation.
    1
    2
    3
    4
    5

13. I have a healthy work environment that supports my well-being.
    1
    2
    3
    4
    5

14. I am satisfied with my physical health and well-being.
    1
    2
    3
    4
    5

15. I am open to seeking professional help or guidance if needed.
    1
    2

3
4
5

Note where you marked low scores, which point to unmet needs. These areas are likely where you need to focus more attention and effort. You may find the following reflection questions helpful in guiding you.

## REFLECTION QUESTIONS

- What did you discover through the self-assessment?
- How can you address specific physical health concerns or challenges in your self-care plan?
- Reflect on recent challenging situations in your work. How did you handle them emotionally?
- What strategies can you implement to enhance your emotional resilience?
- How is your current mental state affecting your work?
- What cognitive challenges have you noticed, and how can you prioritize mental clarity and well-being?

Now that you understand which areas of your life need extra support, it's time to get comfortable with creating and following a program of radical self-care, because your well-being forms the very foundation of your health, happiness, and power.

## CREATING A SUSTAINABLE SELF-CARE ROUTINE

As we embark on our journey toward becoming effective practitioners, let's pause to reflect again on the critical theme of creating a self-care routine. Why do you believe it is essential to transition from sporadic to sustainable self-care?

To guide our reflection, let's explore five reasons why creating a sustainable self-care routine is paramount:

## 1. Long-term resilience

This is our ability to endure and recover from adversity, stress, or challenges over an extended period. It involves developing inner strength, adaptability, and coping mechanisms that allow us to bounce back and maintain our well-being and effectiveness over time.

*How can a sustainable self-care routine help you build resilience and stay committed to the demanding and often emotionally charged field of DEI work?*

## 2. Consistent well-being

Maintaining a regular and balanced approach to self-care practices and lifestyle choices means making deliberate efforts to prioritize physical, mental, and emotional health on an ongoing basis to support overall well-being.

*In what ways will a consistent self-care routine contribute to your personal well-being, allowing you to be a more effective advocate for DEI?*

## 3.Professional effectiveness

This is a person's ability to excel in his or her role or profession. In the context of DEI work, it means being skilled, knowledgeable, and impactful in advocating for diversity, equity, and inclusion within an organization or community.

*How does your well-being impact your professional effectiveness, and what role does a sustainable self-care routine play in this equation?*

## 4. Role modeling

When we role model, we practice setting a positive example for others through our actions, behaviors, and values. This involves demonstrating inclusive practices, empathy, and commitment to inspire and guide others toward a similar mindset and behaviors.

*How can your commitment to sustainable self-care serve as a model for others within your organizations and the DEI field at large?*

## 5. Lasting impact

In the context of DEI, creating a lasting impact means working toward systemic and sustainable change that contributes to greater diversity, equity, and inclusion over an extended period rather than achieving short-term or superficial results.

*What potential exists for your work when you prioritize sustainable self-care as a foundational practice?*

Take some time to reflect on these and the following questions as you continue your journey toward enhancing effectiveness through sustainable self-care. Remember, creating a sustainable self-care routine is not a luxury; it is a necessity. It is a strategic investment in one's ability to ensure personal well-being that will help you navigate the challenges of this work effectively and make lasting change. Sustainable self-care empowers practitioners to be resilient, consistent, and committed advocates for diversity, equity, and inclusion.

## REFLECTION QUESTIONS

- How have your experiences highlighted the need for a sustainable self-care routine in your life?
- Can you recall specific instances when stress or emotional exhaustion impacted your effectiveness as a practitioner? What were the consequences?

- What self-care practices have you previously incorporated into your routine, and how consistent have you been in maintaining them?
- Reflect on a time when you felt overwhelmed or on the verge of burnout. What strategies did you use to recover, and were they sustainable in the long term?
- How do you envision a sustainable self-care routine positively influencing your decision-making and problem-solving abilities?
- What role does creativity play in your work, and how might a consistent self-care routine enhance your creative thinking and problem-solving skills?
- Considering the importance of sustainability in well-being, in what ways can you model and advocate for self-care within your DEI team or community?
- How do you currently balance your commitment to your work with your commitment to self-care? Are there areas where this balance could be improved?
- Reflect on moments in your life when you felt a strong sense of well-being and balance. What self-care practices contributed to those moments, and how can you incorporate them into your current routine?
- What steps can you take to create a sustainable self-care routine that aligns with your unique needs and responsibilities and will help ensure long-term dedication to this vital work?

## SETTING BOUNDARIES

Let's reflect on the valuable insights we gained from chapter 1, where we delved into the pivotal topic of setting boundaries. We took a deep dive into understanding how and why boundaries are essential components of self-care. As we move forward in our journey, it's crucial to carry with us the wisdom and knowledge we gathered in that foundational chapter. These boundary-setting steps will serve as our guiding light, allowing us to navigate this complex landscape with clarity, intentionality, and a steadfast commitment to our well-being.

Healthy boundaries are essential for fostering self-respect, protecting energy, and preventing burnout in both personal and professional realms. They help us maintain balance. Remember, you must get comfortable with saying no with grace and designing and honoring work-life boundaries.

## REFLECTION QUESTIONS

- What are some specific situations in my personal and professional lives where I struggle to set boundaries effectively?
- How do I recognize the signs that I need to set a boundary in a particular situation? What are the physical or emotional cues that signal my discomfort?
- Reflecting on past experiences, can I identify instances where not setting boundaries had a negative impact on my well-being or relationships? What did I learn from those situations?
- What are some strategies or techniques I can employ to communicate my boundaries assertively and respectfully to others?
- How do I handle feelings of guilt or fear that often accompany boundary-setting, especially in professional or social contexts?
- What self-care practices do I need to incorporate into my routine to maintain and reinforce healthy boundaries in my life?
- What are my long-term goals for boundary-setting? How do I envision my life changing or improving as a result of setting and maintaining healthy boundaries?

Congratulations on using your personal experiences to unearth profound insights as you navigate the intricate terrain of self-care and sustainability within your professional journey! Take immense pride in the remarkable work you've accomplished, and continue to embrace the journey ahead with confidence and enthusiasm.

As we conclude this chapter on developing your self-care plan, remember that the path to self-care is a personal and empowering one. You have taken the first steps toward prioritizing your well-being, and that's a commendable achievement.

As you move forward, keep in mind that self-care is not a destination but a continuous journey. Embrace it with an open heart and a commitment to yourself. Remember that self-care is not selfish; it's necessary for your physical, mental, and emotional health.

In the days, weeks, and months ahead, be gentle with yourself. Life can be demanding and challenges may arise, but your self-care plan will serve as your anchor. Take small steps and celebrate your victories, no matter how minor they may seem. Each moment you invest in self-care is an investment in your overall well-being.

Surround yourself with positivity. Enjoy the company of supportive friends and family, engage in activities that bring you joy, or simply take a moment to breathe deeply and reflect. Your self-care plan is your blueprint for resilience, designed to help you navigate the complexities of life with strength and grace.

Lastly, remember that you are worth it. You deserve the love, care, and attention you so readily give to others. By nurturing your own well-being, you are better equipped to show up as your best self in all aspects of your life and the work.

So take this closing moment to reaffirm your commitment to self-care, and with unwavering determination step into the next chapter of your life knowing that you are on the path to greater self-awareness, balance, and fulfillment. Your journey toward self-care is a testament to your strength and resilience. Embrace it with courage, and may your self-care plan be a guiding light leading you to a happier and healthier future.

# CHAPTER 03
## Mental and Emotional Health

It's crucial to understand that harm is harm, and we shouldn't judge or rate someone's suffering. As practitioners, we navigate complex challenges and engage in critical conversations to drive lasting change. The years since the global pandemic, the tragic murder of George Floyd, and the ensuing widespread political, civil, and social unrest have been particularly challenging. A constant barrage of polarizing news cycles filled with hate only adds to the complexity.

While our roles often require us to help organizations address these difficult issues, we sometimes overlook our own well-being. We may place ourselves on the back burner due to the demands of our job and our desire to assist. However, there comes a point when we must prioritize our own mental and emotional health. In an increasingly interconnected world, we're exposed to more harm. I firmly believe that there is no measure of a person's heart; harm is harm, regardless of its form.

Amid these demands, prioritizing mental and emotional well-being is essential. This chapter introduces two key strategies—mindfulness and stress reduction, and seeking professional support—to help practitioners navigate challenges while maintaining their health and sustaining their impact.

## 1. MINDFULNESS AND STRESS REDUCTION

I'll be completely candid here. Mindfulness was a concept I wrestled with for years. When I first heard about it, I imagined sitting alone in a room, attempting yoga and meditation, and quite frankly, I was not interested. My mind would wander in all directions, and instead of feeling calmer, I'd end up more stressed than before. So I sought alternative ways to achieve a sense of mindfulness.

One of my discoveries was journaling, particularly guided journals with reflection questions. As a person of faith, I began allocating time each day for daily devotion and immersing myself in spiritual music, creating playlists that help me navigate my current emotion. Whenever my mind started to drift, I'd gently guide it back—an ongoing struggle that I continue to work on. For someone like me, who is accustomed to a fast-paced, bustling lifestyle, it initially felt uncomfortable, and I even felt guilty for pausing.

But here's the thing I realized: mindfulness doesn't require delving into deep-seated issues or undergoing a radical transformation. It's simply about becoming more self-aware.

My mindfulness practices have been instrumental in reducing stress. I've come to terms with the fact that I might never become a meditation guru, and that's perfectly fine. For me, it's about self-reflection, grounding myself, and asking clarifying questions before my mind races too far ahead.

One practice I find helpful is jotting down my thoughts before bedtime—whatever comes to mind, whether it's important or seemingly trivial. Sometimes I revisit these writings, and sometimes I simply discard them. It's amazing how liberating this process can be. It has brought me closer to myself and to the world around me while reducing the weight of stress.

Mindfulness is a personal journey, and we, as practitioners, must find what works best for us. But it always involves a process of self-discovery. For me, it meant seeking guidance from coaches and counseling to truly understand why spending time with myself felt so daunting. Mindfulness has provided me with a new perspective, helping me appreciate the beauty of the present moment.

Just remember, mindfulness isn't a one-size-fits-all solution. It's about embracing what resonates with us individually and embarking on a journey of self-awareness.

Here are some options for supporting your mindfulness practice:

- **Mindful breathing:** Incorporating brief, mindful breathing exercises into daily routines can help practitioners remain calm during tense meetings or discussions.
- **Meditation and self-reflection:** Regular meditation sessions can foster emotional resilience and provide a space for self-reflection to process challenging interactions.

- **Mindful listening:** Music has the power to bring peace, relaxation, and encouragement. You're welcome to check out my personal playlist in the appendix for inspiration.

## 2. SEEKING PROFESSIONAL SUPPORT

Let's get real for a minute. I'm a big advocate of therapy and seeking help when needed. In the United States, mental health still carries an unfair stigma. It's often brushed aside or seen as a weakness. I'm not a therapist or a doctor, but I've seen my fair share of therapists. I've battled my own demons, struggled with depression, and clawed my way out of its dark depths. It's a tough game, and it's an even greater challenge for those in historically excluded communities. We tend to keep silent about it, especially in the intersectional world of DEI work.

Let me reiterate—I am not a therapist, but I believe therapy or coaching should be a requirement for anyone in this line of work. Why? Because therapy isn't just a nice-to-have; it's a must-have. Therapy is just as vital to our growth as practitioners as any form of professional development.

In fact, I've had therapists tell me something profound: "You can't do this work without a therapist, a coach, or a supportive community." And they were spot on. Our journey involves navigating complex terrains, creating spaces for belonging, and amplifying the voices that often go unheard. To keep our sanity and strength, we need support. And guess what? Seeking help isn't a sign of weakness; it's a testament to our strength and resilience.

Likewise, a dear friend often says, "We're not meant to navigate our careers alone." I couldn't agree more. This work isn't a one-person show. We're here to help organizations and individuals navigate the intricacies of DEI, tackling all the isms of the world. That's why workshops, courses, certifications, and coaching are all part of our toolkits.

But we also need our tribe, a peer support group. These folks know the ins and outs of diversity, equity, inclusion, accessibility, and belonging. They're our kind of people, and they're not afraid to share best practices or lend a supportive ear. There's no need to reinvent the wheel when you have a squad that gets it.

And let's talk conferences. They're not just fun gatherings; they're essential for our growth. I'll let you in on my approach to conferences. I date some, I semi-date a few, and I marry a select group. Confused? Don't worry; I'll break it down for you. When I date a conference, I attend to see what it's all about. I'm there to learn, connect, and soak up knowledge. If it aligns with my goals, both personal and organizational, I keep the relationship going. If not, I move on and explore other opportunities.

Now, marrying a conference is a whole different story. It's a long-term commitment in which we have conversations, partnerships, and a mutual understanding of what we bring to the table. I advocate for them, share leadership, and support them throughout the year. These conferences align with my values and contribute to my professional growth. They're the ones I keep in my corner.

I get it; resources can be tight. But certain organizations that embody my core values are nonnegotiable for me. If your organization invests in industry conferences but not DEI conferences, it's time for a conversation. Your well-being and growth matter.

Later in the book, we'll dive into nonnegotiable core values, which guide and keep us grounded in this work, ensuring that those who care for others are cared for too. Remember, your well-being is an essential foundation for driving meaningful change in the world of diversity, equity, and inclusion.

Here are some examples of structured support:

- **Therapeutic counseling:** Engaging in counseling or therapy sessions can help practitioners process and cope with the emotional toll of their work.
- **Workshops and training:** Participation in workshops or training programs focused on emotional intelligence and stress management equips practitioners with practical skills.
- **Peer support groups:** Joining peer support groups or affinity spaces provides a safe platform for sharing experiences and receiving peer guidance.

# CHAPTER 04
## Physical Well-Being

*All right, let's get real about physical well-being. I've had my fair share of struggles in this department, and let me tell you, it ain't been a cakewalk. This gig is stressful as hell, and there have been times when I let my health take a backseat.*

*But here's the deal, my friend—you can't mess around with your physical well-being. Good health is nonnegotiable. The stress, long hours, and craziness and drama from others will chew you up and spit you out if you don't stand your ground.*

*So I had to call myself out on it. No more excuses, no more putting it off. I had to get disciplined about taking care of my body. Yeah, it meant dragging myself to the gym when I felt like collapsing. It meant saying no to junk food when all I wanted was a burger and fries.*

*But you know what? It's been worth it. I've got more energy, I'm sharper at work, and I can handle the stress better. So if you're in the same boat, don't wait. Get disciplined about your physical well-being, 'cause it's the only body you've got, and this journey ain't for the faint of heart.*

*You've got this!*
*Lois*

## NUTRITION AND EXERCISE

Let's have a real talk about two essential ingredients in the recipe for a healthier you: nutrition and exercise. I've been on a personal journey of renewal since July 22, 2023, and it's a journey that continues every day. After years of being undisciplined about my health, I made the choice to be disciplined about being healthy. Here's what I've learned and some tools to get you started.

## THE IMPORTANCE OF NUTRITION

Nutrition is the fuel that powers your body, and trust me, I know what it's like to struggle with unhealthy choices. One day, as I was getting ready to attend a Beyoncé concert, I found myself frustrated and uncomfortable in everything I put on. I couldn't find anything that made me feel confident. So I decided to go with a pair of jeans and a 2Pac T-shirt.

As I was leaving, my partner jokingly said I looked like Cleo's mugshot from the movie *Set It Off*. That comment hit me hard. It was a turning point, the day I decided to change my life and my relationship with my physical health.

Here are some tools that helped me navigate this ongoing journey:

- **Meal-planning apps:** Tools, such as MyFitnessPal or Lose It!, can help you track your meals, count calories, and monitor nutrients.
- **Healthy-recipe websites:** Websites, such as EatingWell.com, offer a treasure trove of delicious and nutritious recipes to try.
- **Portion-control tools:** Invest in measuring cups and a food scale to help you manage portion sizes.
- **Nutrition books:** There are great books, such as *The China Study* by T. Colin Campbell and *In Defense of Food* by Michael Pollan that provide in-depth insights into healthy eating.
- **Registered dietitian:** Consider consulting with a registered dietitian for personalized guidance on your nutrition journey.

## THE POWER OF EXERCISE

Exercise serves as a fundamental element in promoting both physical health and mental well-being. My personal commitment has led me to the gym rigorously, dedicating a full forty-five minutes to exercise at least six days a week. I must admit, it hasn't been without its daily challenges, but the results have been truly transformative. In this discussion I'll provide you with valuable tools to facilitate your journey toward a healthier lifestyle.

- **Fitness apps:** Apps, such as Nike Training Club, MyFitnessPal, or Fitbit, can create workout plans tailored to your goals.

- **Online workout videos:** Platforms such as YouTube offer a vast selection of free workout videos, from yoga to HIIT.
- **Fitness wearables:** Consider using a fitness tracker or smartwatch to monitor your activity levels and set daily goals.
- **Workout buddy:** Find a workout buddy or join a fitness class for added motivation and accountability.
- **Professional trainer:** If you're unsure where to start, hiring a personal trainer can provide expert guidance.

But here's the real deal—this journey isn't a one-time thing; it's an everyday commitment. I strive to work out every day for at least forty-five minutes, and I make sure to drink a minimum of a gallon of water a day, even though it's tough. I've tapped into expert resources, because, despite being a US Army vet, I knew that I needed help to get back on track.

I'm not ashamed to admit that I've had my slipups and moments of undisciplined living. But what matters is that I hold myself accountable and keep moving forward. This journey is about being healthy, feeling confident, and having energy, not about a number on the scale. I pray every night for better health, but I know it's a daily grind.

I firmly believe that what you put inside your body—whether it's food, reading material, or music—matters. If you put junk in, you get junk out. To do this work, you have to be mindful and give yourself grace. There's no quick fix here; it's about lasting change. This journey is about your health and longevity, and that's worth every step.

## SLEEP HYGIENE

Sleep hygiene is all about cultivating healthy sleep habits to ensure you wake up refreshed and ready to make a positive impact in the world of diversity, equity, and inclusion.

You're on a mission to make the world a more inclusive place, but you're running on empty because of lousy sleep. Sound familiar? Well, here's the deal—sleep hygiene is your secret weapon to recharging and keep crushing it. Here we're breaking down sleep hygiene in a way that offers actionable steps, and I'll share my favorite resources to help you build stellar sleep habits. Trust me, this isn't just personal preference; it's something your health-care provider can vouch for.

## CREATE A CONSISTENT SLEEP SCHEDULE

- **Set your schedule:** Aim for seven to nine hours of quality sleep.
- **Rise with purpose:** Wake up at the same time every day, even on weekends. It sets the tone for an impactful day.
- **No power naps:** Avoid daytime naps, especially in the afternoon. Use that time for meditation or reflection instead; they can be just as invigorating without impacting your nighttime sleep.
- **Stay committed:** Stick to your bedtime schedule, even if you can't doze off right away. Consistency is key for lasting change.

## CREATE A COMFORTABLE SLEEP ENVIRONMENT

- **Chill zone:** Make your bedroom a sanctuary for sleep. Keep it cool (between sixty and sixty-seven degrees F), like you and your ideas.
- **Supportive bed gear:** Invest in a comfy mattress and pillows that support you and your dreams.
- **Dark and quiet:** Create a sleep-worthy environment. Think blackout curtains and white-noise machines.
- **Digital detox:** Ditch screens an hour before bed. Blue light doesn't jibe with your sleep goals.

## MIND WHAT YOU EAT AND DRINK

- **Caffeine control:** Limit afternoon and evening caffeine. It will interfere with a restful night's sleep, which your brain can't function without.
- **Lighten up:** Avoid heavy meals close to bedtime for the same reason. If your day derails and you must eat late, keep your meal light.
- **Happier hydration:** Be sure to stay hydrated during the day, but ease off close to bedtime to minimize midnight bathroom breaks.
- **Snack smarter:** Say no to late-night snacks right before your slumber.

## ESTABLISH A RELAXING BEDTIME ROUTINE

- **Chill mode:** Spend the last hour before bed on calming activities. Think reading, warm baths, or other activities that promote relaxation.
- **Better bedtime:** Create a nighttime routine that signals to your motivated body that it's time to wind down.
- **Stress busters:** Manage daily stress with practices like meditation or deep breathing.
- **Forget the clock:** If you can't sleep, resist the urge to clock-watch. It's not productive for a good night's rest. Instead, try counting classic sheep or backward from 100 to clear your mind.

## FURTHER RESOURCES

- **National Sleep Foundation:** Their website has friendly insights on sleep hygiene and sleep disorders.
- ***Why We Sleep* by Matthew Walker:** A must-read that delves into sleep science and the need for stellar sleep hygiene.

## EFFECTIVENESS OF SLEEP HYGIENE

As a practitioner, your work is essential. To bring your A-game, you need quality sleep. By practicing good sleep hygiene, you'll see improvements in your sleep quality, fewer nighttime interruptions, and a boost in daytime energy and productivity. There is no one-size-fits-all formula, but with some adjustments and patience, you can create sleep habits that elevate your health and therefore your impact. Sleep tight, champion!

# CHAPTER 05

## Inspiring Stories of Self-Care Success

As someone who has been committed to this work for years, I've witnessed firsthand the emotional, mental, and physical toll that DEI practitioners often face. The world was already challenging before 2020, but after George Floyd's murder, the demands placed on DEI professionals grew exponentially. We found ourselves navigating not only our professional responsibilities but deep societal grief and rising tensions.

One personal story that stands out to me involves a period when I was essentially doing two jobs within my organization—managing my day-to-day responsibilities while supporting cultural transformation initiatives. It was during this time that my organization removed a key individual who had created a toxic, unsafe work environment. Shortly after this change, I had an encounter with a colleague who was visibly upset about not being invited to an event. In her frustration, she claimed that my invitations and opportunities within the company were solely because I represented a "picture of diversity." She went on to diminish my accomplishments, reducing me to a symbol rather than recognizing my expertise and dedication.

That conversation stayed with me for a long time. It forced me to question the nature of the opportunities I received. Were they truly based on my capabilities, or was my presence merely a checkmark for diversity? I wrestled with this internal conflict while continuing to pour my energy into client work and my dedication to fostering diversity, equity, and inclusion.

Navigating these external and internal challenges—whether related to politics, race, social dynamics, or gender—often left me without the space to process my own emotions and beliefs. When I first began this work, I thought my role was to change people's beliefs. Over time, I realized this journey is not about changing beliefs but about fostering shared behaviors rooted in respect, accountability, and collective thriving.

I am sharing these stories of self-care success because in the early stages of this work, I did not have a self-care plan. I was working tirelessly without realizing the emotional, mental, and physical toll it was taking. Resilience became an essential part of my survival.

The following stories are from DEI practitioners who, like me, have experienced the importance of prioritizing their well-being. These stories serve as a testament to the power of self-care in sustaining not just our passion but also our effectiveness in creating change.

Remember, we play a crucial role in promoting positive change within organizations and society at large. That means our work can be emotionally and mentally taxing. In this collection of inspiring stories, we explore five scenarios in which prioritizing self-care as an essential part of our journey leads to personal and professional success.

## SARAH'S PERSONAL MINDFUL RETREAT

Sarah knew she was running on fumes when even the smallest tasks felt overwhelming. She had always been the one others turned to for calm guidance, but now, she felt frayed at the edges. The smallest inconvenience sent her spiraling into panic, her emotions raw and unpredictable. She found herself on edge, tears welling at the slightest trigger. It wasn't just exhaustion; it was something deeper. She started dreading interactions, avoided conversations, and retreated from the people she once felt so connected to.

The breaking point came when she arrived home one evening and instinctively hid, unable to face even a simple chat with a friend. That's when she knew—she had to step away. The idea of taking time for herself felt selfish, but the weight pressing down on her told her otherwise. She booked a secluded cabin in the woods, packed a journal, and left, uncertain but desperate for relief.

The mornings were slow, filled with the crisp scent of pine and the distant rustling of leaves. She let herself be still—no expectations, no responsibilities. She breathed. She wrote. She let the silence wrap around her like a balm. Gradually, the tightness in her chest loosened, and the anxious hum quieted.

When she returned, something had shifted. She wasn't magically healed, but she carried a sense of calm she hadn't felt in years. Slowly, she wove those quiet lessons into her work, inviting others to pause, to breathe, and to recognize when they, too, needed to step away.

## MICHAEL'S MENTORSHIP

Michael had always prided himself on being the person who kept everything together, but the weight of constant advocacy began to feel like a mountain pressing down on his chest. Each initiative felt urgent; every meeting brought a new challenge. The pace was relentless. He found himself lying awake at night, thoughts swirling like a storm. One evening, after a particularly hard day, he reached out to a former colleague who had navigated similar struggles. They spoke for hours, not just about strategies but about fears, frustrations, and the loneliness that sometimes accompanies this work. His mentor's advice was simple: "You don't have to carry everything alone." That conversation became the first of many, and Michael began scheduling regular check-ins, not as a task but as a lifeline. The difference was profound—he felt less isolated and more anchored. Slowly, he found himself showing up with more clarity, his passion no longer dulled by exhaustion.

## MARIA'S ARTISTIC OUTLET

Maria's laughter used to fill every room she entered, but over time, it had become quieter, like a song fading out. Her work was meaningful, but she felt like a canvas drained of color. On a whim, she signed up for a local art class. It was messy, joyful, and freeing in ways she hadn't expected. The feel of paintbrushes in her hand brought something within her back to life. Her evenings became an oasis where she painted without expectation, letting her feelings flow in color and form. In those moments, she rediscovered her voice, not in words but in expression. The art didn't just stay on the canvas—it began to influence how she approached her work. Meetings became more dynamic, and her presentations felt alive with fresh ideas. She hadn't just found an outlet; she'd found herself again.

## JAVIER'S COMMUNITY CONNECTION

Javier often felt like a solitary pillar holding up an entire structure. He was committed to supporting others, but who was there to support him? He would stay late at his desk, watching the office empty around him, carrying the weight of stories he had heard from employees who felt unseen and unheard. One day, scrolling through an online forum, he found a local meetup for DEI practitioners. It wasn't fancy—just a group of people gathering at a coffee shop to swap stories and advice. Hesitant but hopeful, Javier attended. The conversations were raw and honest, filled with laughter, shared frustration, and hard-earned wisdom. He left that first meeting feeling lighter, not because his work had changed, but because he was no longer carrying it alone. The community he found became a circle of strength that reminded him he wasn't an island.

## EMMA'S BOUNDARY-SETTING

Emma loved her work, but somewhere along the way she had forgotten how to protect her time. Her calendar was packed from morning to night, her phone constantly buzzing with requests and reminders. She rarely paused, convinced that the work couldn't wait. But her body began sending her messages—headaches, exhaustion, and the nagging feeling that something was missing.

One evening, as she watched her kids play in the yard, she felt a pang of longing. She realized she had been giving her best to her job and only what was left to her family. The next day, she blocked out time on her calendar—not for meetings but for exercise, family dinners, and quiet evenings without screens. At first it felt strange, even selfish, but soon it became a rhythm. Emma's boundaries didn't make her less committed; they made her stronger. She showed up for her team with a renewed sense of purpose, proving that prioritizing herself was one of the most impactful decisions she'd ever made.

These stories remind us that self-care is not a luxury—it is a necessity for sustaining our passion and commitment. Each practitioner had their own fears and reasons for stepping back to prioritize their well-being. But by doing so, they not only improved their personal lives but also became more effective advocates for change. Let these stories serve as an invitation to reflect, recharge, and remember that your well-being is not separate from your impact—it is the foundation of it.

# CHAPTER 06
## Personal Development and Growth

*Hey, good people,*

*I want to open up to you about something very personal. I am a neurodivergent leader with dyslexia, and I've publicly shared about my journey with it. Why am I telling you this? Because it's essential for you to understand that personal and professional development is a path that anyone, regardless of his or her unique challenges, can embark on and succeed in.*

*You already know the importance of investing in yourself. Now I want to emphasize that your organization also should invest in your personal and professional development to support your growth in this ever-evolving field.*

*Throughout this book, we've talked about the significance of wellness and positive mental health. But our work is dynamic and ever-changing, and sometimes we need to adapt to new terms and approaches. We've called it many names over the years—affirmative action, civil rights, DIB, DEI, D&I, EDI, IDEA, JEDI—but at its core, it's all about people. To excel in this role and stay innovative and agile, I've had to engage in continuous self-reflection and develop my skills through various means.*

*This journey hasn't been without its challenges. As a dyslexic writer, crafting this book was a test of determination. I leaned on my family, my board of directors, and my editor for support and guidance. It's shown me that brilliance lies in self-awareness and that personal and professional development is a lifelong journey that demands openness and curiosity.*

*In this section, we'll explore personal development, pushing you to set personal-growth goals, continue learning, and refine your skills. We'll discuss cultivating emotional intelligence, understanding and managing emotions, communicating effectively, building resilience, developing a growth mindset, and leading by example. Remember, people are always watching us, even when we don't realize it. We must foster inclusive teams, set the tone, and be the calm after the storm.*

*Thank you for embarking on this journey of growth and development with me. Let's continue to learn, evolve, and make a lasting impact together.*

*With warmth and understanding,*
*Lois*

## SETTING PERSONAL GROWTH GOALS

In this chapter, we're going to dive deep into the world of personal-growth goals. Many of us work in organizations that conduct annual reviews or should be doing so. These reviews often involve setting organizational goals, which are undoubtedly important. However, it's equally crucial to set personal-growth goals that align with your professional development.

While some of your personal goals may overlap with your organization's or department's objectives, this chapter focuses on your individual growth. As you move through different organizations or roles, you're learning how that organization operates and how to refine yourself as a practitioner in that field. Your personal growth equips you to excel in any organizational context.

Let's take a moment to reflect on your journey as a practitioner. Remember those three questions we explored when developing your personal self-care plan and understanding your whys? You already possess valuable insights into your areas of growth. I'm not asking you to share them with anyone, but I encourage you to use the tools we've discussed in this book to contemplate what you, as a practitioner, need to learn and develop.

Perhaps you're new to this role, transitioning from an ERG leader to a fully dedicated DEI position. Or maybe you've been part of the direct business side of the workforce for years but recently stepped into HR and are grappling with the nuances of this field. Do you comprehend the intricacies of supplier diversity? Can you differentiate between an advisor and a coach? Do you understand how your organization generates revenue? If you're moving from a client-facing role to an HR role, do you grasp the day-to-day experiences of the talent you're supporting?

These are the questions that should be on your radar as a practitioner committed to continuous personal growth. In this chapter, we'll explore the process of setting personal growth goals that align with your evolving role and aspirations. We'll provide examples, strategies, and resources to help you navigate this vital aspect of your professional journey.

So how do we set goals? Well, I'm glad you asked, because I'm going to introduce you to the model I use, which I call the RISE Goal Framework.

## RISE GOAL FRAMEWORK

### R—Relevant (is it relevant to your growth?)

A relevant goal is one that directly connects to your individual development and aspirations. It should be aligned with your personal values and contribute meaningfully to your journey of self-improvement.

**Example:** If you're on a personal-growth journey, a relevant goal might be to improve your communication skills to enhance your relationships with others. This goal is relevant because it directly relates to your personal development and well-being.

### I—Impact (what impact will it have on you?)

An impactful personal growth goal is one that can make a noticeable difference in your life. It's about choosing goals that have the potential to bring about positive change, personal growth, and a sense of fulfillment.

**Example:** Continuing with the previous scenario, if your goal is to improve your communication skills, the impact of achieving this goal could be that you develop deeper and more meaningful connections with friends, family, and colleagues, leading to greater personal satisfaction.

### S—Season (is it the right time for you?)

The right season means considering whether it's the appropriate time in your life to pursue a particular goal. Some goals may be more achievable or relevant at certain times due to personal circumstances, resources, or priorities.

**Example:** If you're currently going through a challenging period of your life, such as dealing with a personal loss or a major life transition, it might not be the right season to take on a complex personal growth goal. It's essential to consider your current circumstances when setting goals.

## E—Evaluate (how can you measure your progress?)

Evaluating a personal growth goal means assessing your progress and determining whether you're moving closer to your desired outcomes. This step is essential for tracking your growth and making necessary adjustments.

**Example:** When working on improving your communication skills, you can evaluate your progress by regularly assessing how well you listen, express yourself, and handle conflicts in your relationships. This self-assessment allows you to measure your growth and adapt your strategies as needed to achieve your goal effectively.

In summary, when setting personal-growth goals using the RISE Goal Framework, consider whether the goal is relevant to your individual development, assess the potential impact it can have on your life, determine if it's the right time in your journey to pursue it, and establish a clear plan for evaluating your progress. This approach ensures that your personal growth goals are meaningful, achievable, and aligned with your path of self-improvement.

# RISE GOAL FRAMEWORK WORKSHEET

Name: _____

Date: _____

**Goal 1**

**R (is it relevant to your growth?)**
Why is this goal important for your personal growth?

**I (what impact will it have on you?)**
How will achieving this goal positively affect your life and personal development?

**S (is it the right time [season] for you?)**
Consider your current situation, commitments, and resources. Is it the right season for this goal?

**E (how can you measure [evaluate] your progress?)**
List specific measures or milestones to track your progress.

    Milestone 1: _____

    Milestone 2: _____

    Milestone 3: _____

Identify steps to achieve your goal.

    1. _____

    2. _____

    3. _____

4. _____

Set a time frame for achieving your goal.

Start date: _____

Target completion date: _____

Choose an accountability partner. Who will support you in achieving this goal?

Name and contact information: _____

## REFLECTION

What steps will you take to reflect on your progress and make adjustments if necessary?

**Goal 2**
(Repeat the RISE Goal Framework for your second goal.)

**Goal 3**
(Repeat the RISE Goal Framework for your third goal.)

This worksheet allows you to set, track, and reflect on three different personal-growth goals using the RISE Goal Framework, providing a comprehensive overview of your goals and action plans.

## ACCOUNTABILITY PARTNERS

Your accountability partner plays a crucial role in your journey toward achieving your personal growth goals. This individual should be someone you trust wholeheartedly. Trust forms the foundation of a successful accountability partnership because you'll be sharing your progress, challenges, and vulnerabilities with them.

However, trust alone is not sufficient. Your accountability partner should also be someone who will hold you accountable and be honest with you. Honesty is a vital component of this relationship because it ensures that the feedback and guidance you receive are genuine and in your best interest.

Here's why trust and honesty are essential in an accountability partner:

- **Confidentiality:** You need to feel safe sharing your goals, setbacks, and personal insights with your partner. Trust ensures that your conversations remain confidential.
- **Effective feedback:** Honest feedback is essential for your growth. Your partner should be comfortable providing constructive criticism when necessary, helping you stay on track and make improvements.
- **Mutual respect:** Trust and honesty go hand in hand with mutual respect. A strong accountability partnership is built on a foundation of respect for each other's goals and aspirations.
- **Supportive environment:** Honesty doesn't mean being harsh or critical; it means providing support in a transparent way. Your partner should encourage and motivate you while also pointing out areas where you can improve.

Remember, your accountability partner should be someone you trust implicitly because you'll be sharing your personal-growth journey with that person. However, he or she should also possess the integrity and courage to provide honest feedback and guidance. This combination of trust and honesty creates a supportive and effective accountability partnership that can significantly enhance your chances of achieving your goals.

## CONTINUOUS LEARNING AND SKILL DEVELOPMENT

Skill development is not a one-time endeavor but a continuous journey. To excel as a practitioner, it is crucial for you to embrace the ethos of lifelong learning and skill development. This chapter explores the importance of continuous learning and provides practical examples of how skill development can enhance your effectiveness.

## WHY CONTINUOUS LEARNING MATTERS

Continuous learning is the cornerstone of personal and professional growth. Here's why it matters:

- **Evolving landscape:** DEI is an ever-evolving field with shifting paradigms, emerging trends, and changing best practices. Staying current is essential to remaining effective.
- **Complex challenges:** The multifaceted challenges in DEI work require a deep understanding of sociocultural dynamics, intersectionality, and systemic issues. Continuous learning equips practitioners to navigate complexity.
- **Adaptive leadership:** Practitioners often serve as change agents within organizations. Continuous learning helps hone leadership skills and enables practitioners to guide organizational transformation effectively.

Here are some examples of continuous learning and skill development:

- **Inclusive leadership training:** Such programs focus on fostering inclusive cultures, leading diverse teams, and addressing bias.
- **Cultural competency workshops:** Courageous Conversation and (Un)learning Space offer workshops that delve into the

complexities of racial equity, which can enhance your understanding of various cultures, perspectives, and experiences.
- **Intersectionality seminars:** Intersectionality Training Institute, She+ Geeks Out, Diversity Builder, and Mission Diverse offer seminars that can deepen your comprehension of the interconnected nature of various identities and how it impacts individuals.
- **Data-analysis courses:** Platforms such as Coursera and edX offer data-analysis courses that can be tailored to DEI applications, such as effectively measuring the impact of our initiatives.
- **Certifications:** The Certified Diversity Professional (CDP) and Certified Diversity Executive (CDE) certifications offered by the Institute for Diversity Certification are recognized in the industry as programs that help validate your expertise and commitment to the field.
- **Mentorship and coaching:** Personalized guidance from experienced DEI practitioners or leaders in your organization can help you develop leadership skills, refine your strategies, and navigate complex challenges.
- **Conferences and webinars:** The National Diversity Council hosts annual conferences that bring DEI professionals together to gain insights from thought leaders, network with peers, and stay informed about industry trends.
- **Reading and research:** Engaging with books, articles, and research papers by authors such as Ibram X. Kendi, Robin DiAngelo, and Kimberlé Crenshaw can provide valuable new perspectives.
- **Community engagement:** DEI-focused communities and affinity groups provide opportunities for learning from peers, sharing best practices, and collaborating on initiatives.
- **Feedback and reflection:** Regularly solicit feedback from colleagues, stakeholders, and the communities you serve to identify areas for improvement.

Continuous learning and skill development are not only about acquiring new knowledge but also about applying that knowledge in meaningful ways. Remember that your commitment to personal growth contributes to the advancement of DEI within your organization and in society at large.

# CHAPTER 07
## Cultivating Emotional Intelligence

Cultivating emotional intelligence is absolutely crucial for success as a DEI practitioner. It starts with a strong sense of self-awareness. To excel in this role, we must deeply understand our own emotions and be adept at recognizing those of others, all while effectively managing these emotions to foster better communication and empathy within the organization.

Emotional intelligence has been discussed extensively, with studies, assessments, and experts dedicated to it. And it is vital that we take the time to delve into this subject. It should find a place in all of our personal development plans. I've personally taken numerous courses, read various books (the titles of which I've included in the appendix), and constantly peruse articles on emotional intelligence.

In my experience, strong emotional intelligence has offered one of the most effective ways to gain traction in DEI work. It's what has helped me navigate challenging conversations and engage allies. For me, this journey has been about understanding and identifying my own triggers and biases and recognizing how they impact my work. It's enabled me to assess whether I'm bringing my best self to a situation and being objective or if my biases and personal beliefs are clouding my judgment. Remember, we're all human, so while we guide others through their journeys, we're also on our own path of discovery.

When it comes to nurturing emotional intelligence, there are three vital areas to focus on:

> understanding and managing our emotions;
> communicating effectively; and
> showing empathy.

Grasping our emotions and learning how to handle them is a lifelong journey. It requires introspection, support, and openness to change. It's hard but important work for leaders of all kinds.

Effective communication is absolutely key. It's the golden thread that runs through everything we do. Whether it's a team meeting or a company-wide email, how we express ourselves can make or break our efforts. I've personally struggled with written communication due to dyslexia, but I've found that technology and a supportive team can work wonders in getting the message across clearly and powerfully.

And then there's empathy. To me, empathy is about understanding others' feelings without necessarily having to walk in their shoes. It's about being respectful and open to different perspectives while still holding true to your own values.

In essence, this work is about building a culture of mutual respect and understanding. It's not about changing personal beliefs, but about creating a shared behavior that respects everyone. This approach is crucial, especially as we navigate the complex and often controversial issues that always lie ahead to create a space where everyone feels valued and can contribute their best. So how do we do this? I'd like to share my steps with you.

## MANAGING EMOTIONS

Understanding and managing often messy emotions is crucial in creating a more inclusive and empathetic environment. Here are three accessible steps to help you and others do so effectively.

1. **Self-reflection:** Begin by acknowledging your own emotions. Take time to reflect on what you're feeling and why. Recognize that all emotions are valid and normal. Consider how your emotions might affect your behavior and decisions in DEI efforts.

    Here are some key self-reflection questions:

    - **What triggered this emotion?**
      This question helps you identify the specific event or situation that brought up the emotion, allowing you to better understand the root cause.

    - **How is this emotion affecting my thoughts and behaviors?**
      Self-reflection can help you recognize how your emotions are influencing your actions and decisions, which is important for managing them effectively.

- **What can I do to address or cope with this emotion in a healthy way?**
  This question encourages you to think about constructive strategies for dealing with the emotion, whether it's engaging in relaxation techniques, seeking support, or taking a break to process your feelings.

2. **Active listening:** When interacting with others, particularly in DEI discussions, practice active listening. Give people your full attention, ask clarifying questions, and validate their emotions. Try to put yourself in their shoes to understand their perspective and experiences.

Here are some useful examples of clarifying questions:

- **Could you please elaborate on that point?**
  This question encourages the speaker to provide more details or examples, helping you gain a deeper understanding of their perspective.

- **I want to make sure I'm following you correctly; are you saying (repeat their main point)?**
  Repeating their main point and asking for confirmation ensures that you've accurately understood their message.

- **What do you mean when you say (use a specific term or phrase they used)?**
  This question seeks clarification on any terms or jargon the speaker has used, preventing misunderstandings and promoting effective communication.

3. **Emotional regulation:** Develop techniques to regulate your own emotions. This could include deep breathing, mindfulness exercises, or taking short breaks when needed. Recognize when you're becoming overwhelmed and take steps to calm yourself before reacting impulsively.

Through these steps, I've managed to boost my capacity, effectively handle my emotions, minimize frustration, and avoid burnout. It all boils down to my ability to maintain boundaries. Additionally, I've also shared these steps within my team, which has helped them understand their own emotions in challenging situations, improve their communication, and foster psychologically safe and inclusive working environments.

## EFFECTIVE COMMUNICATION AND EMPATHY

We're all aware that effective communication is the beating heart of our work, be it through spoken words or written messages, addressing our internal teams or reaching out to the wider world. We've all found ourselves in conversations that are emotionally charged, are polarizing, or touch on controversial topics. That's why it's crucial to tackle these discussions with authenticity, empathy, and inclusivity in mind.

Let me break down the four practical steps I consistently follow:

1. **Establish a trusted advisor network:** I've built a network of trusted advisors within and outside my organization, valuing diversity in their perspectives and backgrounds. I lean on them for guidance, feedback, and support when navigating complex or emotionally charged topics. Their insight helps me recognize the value of different viewpoints, approach discussions with empathy and improve my efficacy.
2. **Practice authenticity and inclusive language:** When addressing polarizing or controversial topics, I prioritize authenticity, staying true to my values and DEI principles. I use inclusive language that respects the diversity of my audience and helps me to empathize with their experiences and perspectives. These are the keys to building trust and fostering open conversations.
3. **Be prepared and find clarity:** I understand that preparation is essential. Before engaging in discussions, I thoroughly research the topic, gather relevant data, and anticipate potential objections or concerns. This way I approach conversations with

clarity, presenting my points confidently and with conviction. This clarity helps me build a strong foundation for productive dialogue. I use "I" statements to express my thoughts and feelings authentically, always keeping empathy at the forefront.
4. **Rely on integrity and honesty:** I hold integrity and honesty in high regard, understanding that these principles are closely tied to empathy. Consistently upholding these values builds trust among my colleagues and stakeholders, as they know they can rely on my words and actions.

One of the most important lessons I've learned is that anything I communicate internally may quickly become external. Therefore, I remain vigilant in my communication practices, ensuring they align with my values and the organization's DEI goals. While effective communication can be challenging, especially in emotionally charged contexts, I know that by consistently applying these practices rooted in empathy, I am creating a more inclusive and equitable environment, driving meaningful change within my organizations and communities.

# CHAPTER 08
## Building Resilience

*Hey, y'all,*

*I want to take a moment to chat with you about the art of resilience. It's a quality that's been a loyal companion and a demanding teacher, challenging me in ways I could never have imagined. In this role, amid all its challenges, what keeps me steady is my unwavering commitment to the work we do and the tangible impact it has had, not just within the organizations I've served but far beyond.*

*For me, resilience is more than just bouncing back from adversity; it's about evolving, learning, and growing from every experience. Whether I'm facing a minor setback or a massive roadblock, staying true to my principles and values is paramount, especially when shit inevitably hits the fan. Resilience gives me the strength to persevere in the face of resistance, knowing the importance of our work.*

*I often reflect on the numerous times my resilience has been tested. The long, often challenging conversations, the resistance to change, and the emotional toll that accompanies advocating for historically excluded voices—these moments can be quite the trial. Yet it's in these very moments that I've discovered the deepest wellsprings of my resilience. I know that failing to advocate and hold people accountable can lead to harm, whether intentional or not. And while I can't prevent all harm, I can establish boundaries and an accountability framework to address it when it arises.*

*What continually fuels my resilience is witnessing the impact of my efforts—the stories of individuals within our organization whose lives have been transformed for the better and the knowledge that our work ripples out, touching lives far beyond our immediate workplace. But here's the truth: I didn't build this resilience on my own. It's been nurtured and strengthened through partnerships with colleagues who share the same dedicated commitment to change. Together, we've provided unwavering support, leaning on one another when the weight of our mission felt almost too heavy to bear. These relationships have been my anchor, reminding me that I'm not alone on this journey.*

*My role as a voice for those who are often voiceless and unheard is an enormous privilege and a responsibility that keeps me grounded. It's the understanding that our work has the power to create a world where every voice is valued—where equity is not just an aspiration but a living reality—that keeps me moving forward.*

*So as we navigate the ever-evolving DEI landscape, I want to express my heartfelt gratitude for the resilience that has carried us through. Together, we'll keep moving forward, learning from each challenge and striving for a future where inclusion and equity are the guiding principles that shape our world.*

*With dedication and warmth,*
*Lois*

In the ever-evolving landscape of DEI, resilience is not merely a desirable trait; it's an essential asset. As I delve into the subject of building resilience in this chapter, I find myself reflecting on the profound role faith and unwavering commitment have played in my journey.

In a climate where many of my esteemed colleagues have departed from this challenging and often turbulent field, where organizational commitments have seen rollbacks, and where the worth of our work is continually scrutinized, I've remained steadfast. What has kept me committed, even during times of doubt and uncertainty? It's my profound belief in the transformative potential of DEI initiatives—a belief that has been fortified by the remarkable impact I've witnessed within the organizations I support and beyond.

My family, too, has played a pivotal role in sustaining my commitment. Their constant support, encouragement, and understanding have been my bedrock. As the tides have shifted, they've stood by me, reminding me of the importance of my mission and the difference I've made—and have yet to make.

I've often found myself in the unique position of being the first person organizations lean on when the waters become turbulent. It's a role that carries immense responsibility but just as much satisfaction. Especially as we navigate a polarizing times, both in the United States and across the world, marked by divisions and fears, I find solace in knowing that I am a voice for the often faceless and unheard within the workplace.

Maintaining resilience in such a demanding environment requires more than just determination; it necessitates a deep sense of self. As you navigate through these pages, I'll share how cultivating a strong sense of self has been instrumental in keeping me grounded, even in the face of adversity.

Throughout this book and particularly in this chapter, I continue to encourage you to cultivate a growth mindset. Challenges and adversaries will undoubtedly emerge, but it's in these moments that we have the greatest opportunity for growth and transformation. I invite you to explore the strategies and insights I've gathered on building resilience and nurturing a commitment that withstands the test of time. Together, we'll uncover how to navigate the DEI journey with fortitude and grace.

## OVERCOMING ADVERSITY

I've come to understand that the greatest challenges in this work often stem from fears of change, loss, and being labeled. I firmly believe it's imperative to meet people where they are. It's heartening that a significant number of people are eager to engage in this work, but we must also remember that we are dealing with longstanding and deep-seated issues—the isms that have existed since time immemorial. For many, discussing topics like race, religion, or politics in the workplace is new and uncomfortable territory. Traditionally, these subjects were kept separate from the professional environment. But now they are increasingly becoming part of office conversations.

Additionally, we are in a unique time in work history where multiple generations are present in the workforce, each with its own perspective on work-life balance and the employee-organization relationship. In navigating these complexities, the key to overcoming adversity and challenges lies in keeping an open mind, being genuinely curious, and approaching situations with a blend of accountability and grace. Overcoming challenges and adversity is not just about tackling immediate issues; it's about developing resilience, finding creative solutions, and maintaining a positive outlook amid these difficulties. This approach is universally applicable, especially for those of us who frequently navigate these intricate and challenging scenarios.

The following four-step guide offers a structured approach to these challenges.

## 1. Acknowledge and analyze the challenge

In my experience, the first step is always to acknowledge the challenge I'm facing. For instance, when I rolled out a new mentorship program specifically designed for our BIPOC talent, the backlash was as intense as a skillet of catfish frying in hot grease. I was more than a little pissed to encounter such resistance. But instead of boiling over, I stepped back to cool down and really understand the reasons behind this pushback and its impact on our organizational goals. I had to ask myself, "What's the real issue here?" and "How does this intersect with our DEI objectives?"

This wasn't just about uncovering a problem; it was an opportunity to learn and grow. I learned there was an underlying fear that if we didn't open the mentorship to everyone, we'd be seen as playing favorites. By taking a step back, I could address everyone's concerns without losing my cool.

## 2. Seek support and leverage resources

I've realized the significance of collaboration and seeking guidance. When facing challenges or adversaries, I lean on the wisdom of mentors and the experience of colleagues, because nine out of ten times, they've experienced the same or a similar issue. This collaborative spirit extended even to the early stages of this book and its design. I consulted a circle of trusted advisors—board members, seasoned practitioners, and some of the sharpest minds distanced from my field. Their insights were invaluable, offering perspectives I might have missed.

Remember the words of my dear friend who also serves on my advisory board: "We're not meant to journey through our careers alone." This sentiment resonates deeply with me. As a woman with dyslexia, I embrace tools such as Grammarly and voice-to-text for clear communication, and

I keep a traditional dictionary on my desk and an app on my phone for quick reference. I'm an avid reader who delves into books across various subjects, and I tune in to many podcasts—there's no need to reinvent the wheel when wisdom is already out there.

When it comes to overcoming challenges to the work, I actively seek out training sessions and webinars. Reflecting on questions like, "Who in my circle can offer insights?" and "Which resources can best address this challenge?" helps me construct a solid foundation of support and arm myself with essential tools for success.

## 3. Develop and Communicate a Clear Strategy

I understand the importance of having a well-crafted strategy and communicating it clearly at all levels of an organization. In our field, where we often encounter scrutiny and polarization, effective communication is absolutely necessary.

I firmly believe that prioritizing this communication is the foundation of effective strategy. It's about ensuring that everyone, from our executive leadership to individual contributors, knows what we're doing and understands the why and how behind our initiatives. This approach fosters an environment of inclusivity within the strategy itself, reducing misunderstandings, and creating a shared commitment to our goals.

While formulating a clear strategy is essential, it's equally important to document and communicate it effectively throughout the organization. When implementing programs or initiatives, I make it a priority to clearly articulate the plan to those leading the charge, demonstrating how it aligns with our overarching DEI strategy and objectives. I'm always ready to break it down step-by-step to ensure a thorough understanding of how each element contributes to our mission.

In the dynamic landscape of this work, flexibility is key. I'm open to adjusting our approach and programming as needed, but our core strategy remains steadfast unless it no longer serves our business objectives or strategies. I regularly reflect on and reevaluate my actions, asking myself if they align with our goals and what changes might be necessary to enhance our strategy. This ongoing scrutiny ensures that my efforts remain focused, intentional, and impactful.

## 4. Maintain a growth mindset

Let's keep it real, folks. Naming this section had me scratching my head for a bit. I thought about going with "Develop a Growth Mindset," but truth be told, in this line of work you can't just build one from scratch. You gotta bring it with you. If you don't, you might find yourself lagging behind, and maybe this ain't your calling.

Yep, you heard me—I'm laying it out there. If that growth mindset ain't already in your toolbox, it might be time to explore other career avenues. I mean, seriously, that's the deal.

So I settled on "Maintain a Growth Mindset," because, let me tell you, this journey is full of challenges that'll test your mettle. Personally, I'm always on the hustle to keep that growth mindset alive and kicking. As you know, I'm all about reflection. I make sure my team and I break it down after every event, every initiative, every program. What could we have done better? What's the takeaway for next time? Even the tough conversations—I approach 'em with a healthy dose of curiosity.

Maintaining a growth mindset is at my core. Whether a project goes off without a hitch or hits a few bumps, there's always a lesson to learn. I ask myself, "What did I gain from this experience?" and "How can I apply that wisdom moving forward?" It's all about embracing every moment as a chance to level up, both personally and professionally.

# CHAPTER 09
## Psychological Safety

*Hey there,*

*I want to have a real talk with you about something that's at the heart of what we do: psychological safety. Let me be straight with you—it's pretty much one of the most crucial parts of our gig. If we don't have that sense of security and freedom within our organization, we've gotta ask ourselves the hard question: Is this place really for us?*

*We're gonna dive into the nitty-gritty of psychological safety. We'll explore what it actually is, and how you can nurture it in your team and throughout your organization—how to forge the essential relationships that create a safe space.*

*But hold up. Before we get into all that, let's take a moment for a bit of self-reflection. We're gonna do a little exercise to gauge how mentally safe we feel in our current roles. It's important to be honest with ourselves here.*

*And hey, if after this assessment you find that your mental safety isn't quite where it needs to be, don't stress. I've got your back. We're gonna work through this together, and I'll guide you through how to ground yourself and figure out the next steps. Because remember, at the end of the day, you deserve to be in a place that values and supports your mental well-being.*

*Let's get to it and make sure we're all in the right headspace to do our best work.*

*Catch you in the next chapter,*
*Lois*

## PSYCHOLOGICAL SAFETY DEFINED

Mental safety in our workplaces is crucial—it's the foundation of a vibrant and successful organizational culture. It's about crafting a space where you can be yourself, speak up, share your innovative ideas and strategies, and address problems without the dread of being disrespected or penalized. Pioneered twenty-five years ago by Harvard Business School professor Amy Edmondson, the concept of psychological safety is simple yet profound: when people feel safe to take risks and know their workplace is supportive, they perform better.

According to Edmundson's 1999 research study, a psychologically safe workplace is one that's stripped of fear, humiliation, and negativity. In a space where creativity, strategic thinking, and teamwork are allowed to flourish, you see the real magic of diversity and inclusion at play.

And remember Google's Project Aristotle? It showed us that psychological safety is not just nice to have—it's a must-have for teams to thrive. It fosters a place where everyone is encouraged to put forward ideas, embrace and learn from mistakes, and bolster each other's strengths and weaknesses.

## PSYCHOLOGICAL SAFETY ASSESSMENT

Reflect on the following seven questions honestly, and rate your comfort level for each on a scale from 1 (not at all) to 5 (completely). This will help you gauge the level of psychological safety you currently experience in your role. If you find that your scores are leaning toward the lower end of the scale, it may be an indicator that your workplace's psychological safety needs attention, and it might be time to explore strategies to improve it or consider whether the environment aligns with your needs for mental well-being. So grab your notebook, and let's dive in.

## REFLECTION QUESTIONS

1. **Voice and contribution**
   - Do I feel comfortable speaking up and contributing my ideas during meetings?
   - Can I express my thoughts without fear of ridicule or harsh judgment from my colleagues or superiors?

2. **Errors and learning**
   - How do I feel when I make a mistake at work? Is it treated as a learning opportunity, or is it held against me?
   - Am I able to admit to errors without fear of negative repercussions?

3. **Support and respect**
   - Do I feel that my colleagues and leadership support me and show respect for my opinions?
   - When I share personal accomplishments or challenges, do I receive a supportive and empathetic response?

4. **Inclusion and diversity**
   - Do I believe that my unique perspective is valued on my team, and do I feel included in all aspects of team dynamics?
   - Are diversity and individual differences celebrated and taken into account when decisions are made in my workplace?

5. **Feedback and growth**
   - Is the feedback I receive constructive and aimed at my growth rather than critical and discouraging?
   - Do I feel that my personal and professional development is a priority for my organization?

6. **Trust and integrity**
   - Do I trust my leaders and colleagues to act with integrity and in the best interests of the team?
   - Am I confident that confidential information I share will be handled appropriately?

7. **Work-life balance**
   - Does my workplace culture respect my personal time and promote a healthy work-life balance?
   - Am I able to set boundaries regarding my availability without fear of it impacting my job security or opportunities for advancement?

Hey, how are you feeling after going through that assessment? It can be quite an eye-opener to reflect on these aspects of our work lives, right? I want you to consider a few things: Did any questions make you feel uneasy or particularly comfortable? Were there any surprises about your current work environment that came to light? And most importantly, how does this reflection align with what you truly want from your professional life?

Now, take a moment to step back and process everything. Here's a reminder of the tools we introduced early in the book to help you digest your thoughts and feelings:

- **Journaling:** Grab a notebook and jot down your initial reactions to the assessment. Writing can help you process your emotions and clarify your thoughts.
- **Mindfulness meditation:** Spend some time in quiet reflection or meditation. This can aid in managing any stress or anxiety that may have surfaced and bring you to a place of calm.
- **Walk in nature:** If possible, go for a walk outside. Nature has a way of soothing the mind and giving us a fresh perspective on things.
- **Talk to a trusted friend or mentor:** Sometimes speaking with someone who knows you well can provide comfort and insight, helping you to sort through your feelings.

Remember, these results are for and about you. They're a starting point for understanding where you stand in terms of mental safety in your current role and what your next steps might be. Take all the time you need; this is your journey and well-being at stake.

So after taking this assessment, regardless of your results, know this: You're now equipped with knowledge about where you stand. Whether you're basking in a psychologically safe environment or recognizing areas that need improvement, this understanding is your first step toward fostering a healthier workplace. As DEI practitioners, we leverage this insight to champion change and cultivate spaces where everyone can soar.

If your current workspace doesn't exactly scream safe haven, don't sweat it. Remember those nifty tricks we chatted about in the first part of the book? They're like your secret weapon in these situations.

All right, so let's break it down into four smooth steps for when you're feeling more office outcast than office MVP:

1. **Find your tribe:** Spot those kindred spirits at work who also want to make things better. Link up and start spreading the good vibes. It's all about that team spirit.
2. **Set your boundaries:** Let people know what's cool with you and what's not. Got an issue? Talk it out with someone who can help make a difference—just keep it respectful.
3. **Self-care is key:** Don't let the job grind you down. Whether it's yoga, a good book, or just kicking back with your favorite show, make sure you're keeping your batteries charged.
4. **Keep your receipts:** When things go south, like if you spot harassment or bias, jot it down—what went down, when it happened, and who was involved. This isn't just for the drama; it's about having the facts straight when you chat with HR or the party involved to sort things out.

And don't forget, if it feels like you're banging your head against a brick wall and it's time for a change, that's cool too. Sometimes the best place to be is somewhere new, and in chapter 20 I'll walk you through how to get there responsibly. Keep your head high—you've got this!

## IMPORTANCE OF PSYCHOLOGICAL SAFETY

As a practitioner, I find myself in the unique position of being a guardian of safety for the talent within my organization. I am often the confidant, the mediator, and the advocate. It's a role I approach with the utmost care and responsibility, understanding that the environment I help to shape can significantly influence the well-being and productivity of our team members.

Aside from the policymaking, program design, and training sessions, it's in the quiet conversations and shared stories where the foundation of trust is built. We often become keepers of confidence, providing a space where individuals can be vulnerable without fear—a space where they can share not just their successes but their struggles and uncertainties.

Being a role model in fostering a safe environment is a responsibility I take seriously. This role requires me to listen actively, communicate effectively, empathize deeply, and act with integrity. For instance, I recall collaborating with a team member who felt hesitant to share ideas, stemming from experiences where this person's contributions were overlooked. I consciously made an effort to highlight their input during meetings, reinforcing that their perspectives were not only welcome but highly valued. Such a mindful act contributed to transforming the team's dynamics, cultivating a culture where each member felt encouraged to contribute openly.

But here's the real talk: While we're busy creating safe spaces for others, we must not forget to secure our own psychological safety. We cannot pour from an empty cup. I remember a time when I was navigating a particularly challenging project that required difficult conversations around bias and inclusion. While I was supporting others, I found myself feeling isolated. It was a moment of realization—I needed to seek my own safe space. I reached out to a mentor, which helped me regain my footing and reinforced the importance of having my own safe harbor within the workplace.

In crafting these environments, we're doing more than just ticking off a checklist. We're cultivating a garden where diversity thrives, ideas bloom, and the fruits of our labor are the advancements we see in our organization's culture and the well-being of its people. While we're building these spaces for others, we need to ensure we're also standing on solid ground.

To all you dedicated practitioners out there, here are a few tips for building psychological safety within your organizations. But before you dive in, ensure that your organization is primed for change and that you're operating from a place of security. When applied in a ready and receptive environment where you feel secure and valued, these steps are transformative.

## CREATING PSYCHOLOGICAL SAFETY

- **Encourage participation in decision-making:** Invite team members to be part of the decision-making process. For example, use collaborative tools for brainstorming sessions where everyone can add their ideas asynchronously before coming together to discuss them.
- **Provide personalized encouragement:** Take note of individual team members' strengths and acknowledge them. If people are struggling, offer specific, constructive feedback and the chance to work on projects that play to their strengths, which can boost their confidence and sense of belonging.
- **Clarify roles and responsibilities:** Ensure everyone knows their role and how it contributes to the team's or organization's larger goals. Use regular check-ins to help team members understand their impact, which can help prevent misunderstandings and conflict.
- **Champion equity and accessibility:** Actively seek out and remove barriers to participation. This might mean providing translation services for nonnative speakers or ensuring that all meeting locations are accessible for team members with disabilities.

## NAVIGATING DIFFICULT CONVERSATIONS

Let's chat about something that's become a big slice of our daily grind—those tricky talks that can feel like you're navigating a minefield. And let's be real: Since the world got turned upside down with the murder of George Floyd, the social storms that followed, and the whole global pandemic, our jobs have been packed to the brim with these kinds of moments.

Every time you flick on the news, there's a crisis or heartache that spills over into our work lives. We're on the front lines, trying to make sense of it all, while helping others do the same. It's part of the gig, sure, but it doesn't make it any less heavy.

And let's not skirt around the fact that not everyone is down with change or sees eye to eye on what's happening. There are folks who struggle with differences, and sometimes we're the ones they vent to when they feel the organization isn't moving in the direction they think it should.

So how do we handle it? First, we've got to stay in the know, because knowledge is our armor. Listen with intent, and remember, taking a deep breath can go a long way toward keeping your cool and ultimately maintaining your balance. It's OK to hit the pause button and collect your thoughts.

After the dust settles on these tough convos, make sure you take care of you. Find your Zen, your quiet place, your jam—whatever helps you bounce back. Because in this whirlwind of change and challenge, safeguarding our sanity isn't just nice, it's necessary.

Buckle up, friends—it's a wild journey we're on, but believe me, we're equipped with the right gear to steer through it. Let's dive in.

I'm going to lay out the steps that have been my go-tos for owning these conversations. And trust me, whenever I've rolled with these, I've walked away pretty unscathed. Now, I'll keep it real with you—there are times when these tough talks get me so riled up, I'm just about ready to throw down. But then I hear my grandma's voice in my head, reminding me, "You catch more bees with honey than with vinegar." So let's sweet-talk our way through this, shall we?

- **Strategize and equip:** Arm yourself with knowledge about the subject matter at hand before engaging in a challenging discussion. Anticipate potential inquiries and prepare relevant examples and feedback. For instance, when addressing performance, be ready with clear instances and positive guidance.
- **Maintain composure:** Cultivate a composed presence throughout intense exchanges. Utilize techniques such as deep breathing to retain equanimity if the conversation escalates.

- **Engage and acknowledge:** Demonstrate engagement by paraphrasing the speaker's points and recognizing their sentiments. When delivering feedback that may be difficult to receive, acknowledge the employee's perspective to show your understanding.
- **Pursue joint resolutions:** Aim to collaboratively uncover solutions. In the event of a dispute among team members, orchestrate a mediation effort that invites input and consensus from all involved parties.

As we work toward establishing a psychologically secure atmosphere by managing challenging dialogues, our ultimate aim is to foster an environment rich in understanding, empathy, and mutual respect in which each team member feels acknowledged and valued.

In both creating a safe environment and navigating tough talks, the goal is to enhance understanding, empathy, and respect within teams and organizations, ensuring that every individual feels seen, heard, and valued.

# CHAPTER 10
## Physical Safety

As we delve into the nuanced world of DEI, it's essential to address a component that often operates silently in the backdrop—our physical safety. The very act of advancing DEI can nudge us into sensitive areas, stirring emotions and potentially unsettling the security we often take for granted.

Advocacy, by its nature, can invoke a spectrum of reactions. Not everyone is aligned with the path to change, and tensions can escalate quickly. This reality makes it imperative that our work environments are equipped with not just supportive cultures but also concrete, actionable safety measures.

A secure workplace is foundational to our ability to perform effectively. From access controls to emergency protocols, knowing that our organization supports our physical safety empowers us to advocate boldly and confidently.

## INCLUSIVE SAFETY AT WORK

To ensure our safety and the safety of those we advocate for, here are the measures we should advocate for in our workplaces:

- **Robust security:** Ensure we have secure access to our workspaces, necessary surveillance, and a contingency plan for unforeseen events.
- **Clear-cut policies:** Advocate for unambiguous policies detailing acceptable conduct and explicit procedures for addressing violations.
- **Preparedness training:** Regularly participate in safety drills and training on de-escalating tense situations.
- **Protected reporting:** Establish a confidential system for reporting any threats or incidents that safeguards the reporter's privacy.
- **Responsive measures:** Ensure that any reported incidents are taken seriously and addressed promptly and effectively.

Advocating for inclusive workspaces includes advocating for our own safety. If we perceive a risk, it's our right and responsibility to voice our concerns. And should an incident occur, documenting the details is a crucial step toward ensuring a proper response and preventing future occurrences.

## TAMELA'S STORY: A CONSULTANT CONFRONTS AN UNREADY ORGANIZATION

Tamela, a seasoned DEI consultant, arrived at a growing firm with a cautious sense of optimism. On paper, the company had professed its commitment to diversity and inclusion—but they'd done little to prepare managers or employees for the realities of a genuine DEI conversation. Tamela expected some degree of pushback, as she knew from experience that DEI efforts can unsettle established power structures. Still, she hadn't anticipated the intensity of resistance that she would encounter.

Midway through her presentation on gender diversity, an employee named Mark confronted her with an aggressive tirade, dismissing the workshop as "biased and unnecessary." He refused to engage with the data and real-life examples Tamela presented, shutting down any chance for a respectful exchange. A few coworkers joined in with eye-rolls and interruptions, seemingly relieved someone else had voiced their own skepticism. Tension mounted, and before long, the atmosphere in the room grew hostile.

The HR team on-site tried to intervene, but their lack of training became glaringly obvious. Instead of redirecting the conversation or setting ground rules, they allowed Mark's outburst to dominate the session. Tamela felt her professional and personal safety eroding by the minute. She had come to facilitate a learning experience, not endure an onslaught on her credibility.

After the workshop, Tamela debriefed with HR, explaining that lasting DEI improvements require foundational practices like consistent, open communication channels and protocols for handling dissent. She emphasized the importance of leadership accountability—how visible support from top executives could set a strong example for everyone else. Yet, HR managers were hesitant to address the issue directly, fearing further backlash from a vocal minority. In the end, they took no meaningful steps, leaving Tamela's suggestions on the table.

Realizing the firm lacked the resolve to embrace genuine change, Tamela decided to end her engagement. She'd done what she could, but progress demanded organizational buy-in—something clearly missing here. Though disappointed, she knew her expertise deserved a setting that wouldn't let hostility stand unchallenged. In her final report, she reiterated that readiness is nonnegotiable. If a company truly wants to foster an inclusive culture, it must prepare to confront discomfort, set strong policies, and back up its objectives with real action.

Walking away felt bittersweet, yet it underscored a crucial lesson: Advocating for diversity, equity, and inclusion can only go so far in an environment unwilling to confront its own resistance. By prioritizing her own safety and integrity, Tamela affirmed that every DEI consultant—and every champion of inclusion—deserves a workplace ready to do the work it claims to believe in.

## ALEX'S CRISIS-READY STAND FOR INCLUSIVITY

For Alex, serving as the social media manager for a popular fashion brand was both thrilling and high-pressure. The company had built its reputation around celebrating diversity—showcasing models of different sizes, backgrounds, and identities in its campaigns. One day, Alex launched a new initiative featuring a plus-size, nonbinary model under the tagline "All Bodies, All Stories," believing it would spark meaningful conversations. And it did—but not all of them were positive.

At first, the response was overwhelmingly supportive. Customers and followers applauded the bold move, sharing stories of how seeing themselves represented made them feel seen and valued. But as the post gained traction, pockets of backlash began to emerge. Some critics posted hurtful comments, questioning the brand's motives and ridiculing the model's identity. Within hours, it escalated into personal attacks, threats, and boycotts. Alex was stunned by the virulence but knew he had to act quickly before the negativity overshadowed the campaign's inclusive message.

Thankfully, the company had a well-established crisis response plan—something Alex had only seen references to in the employee handbook. The moment the hateful comments and threats started rolling in, senior leadership sprang into action. They formed a cross-functional team that included PR, legal counsel, security experts, and Alex as the social media lead.

- **Security measures:** The security team immediately briefed Alex on best practices for handling online threats, including reporting procedures for law enforcement if personal safety became a concern. They also reminded staff to tighten their social media privacy settings.
- **Unified messaging:** PR prepared official statements reinforcing the brand's commitment to inclusivity, while Alex and the content team drafted responses that balanced compassion with firm boundaries against hateful language. The brand publicly reaffirmed that the campaign was a reflection of its core values, not a marketing stunt.
- **Executive support:** Perhaps most crucially for Alex's peace of mind, senior executives personally praised him for spearheading the campaign and made it clear they wouldn't back down or apologize for promoting diversity. The CEO even recorded a short internal video encouraging employees to stand behind the campaign, reminding them that hateful voices, while loud, don't represent the majority.

Throughout it all, Alex felt an unexpected sense of reassurance. Instead of being left to fend off trolls alone or asked to scale back the campaign, he was supported every step of the way. The swift mobilization made it clear that diversity wasn't just a buzzword for the brand—it was an operational principle, embedded in how they responded to crises.

Within a few days, the situation stabilized. Negative comments still trickled in, but the company's proactive stance and strong public messaging had largely neutralized the worst of the backlash. More importantly, Alex emerged from the ordeal feeling valued—both as an employee and as someone tasked with carrying out a mission that aligned with his personal convictions.

This experience underscored just how pivotal organizational readiness can be in DEI work. A less prepared company might have distanced itself from the campaign or silenced Alex to avoid controversy. But here, decisiveness and principled action validated the importance of representation and gave Alex the confidence to continue pushing for inclusion. It was a powerful reminder that safety—both emotional and professional—isn't just about having protocols in place; it's also about having leaders willing to defend those protocols when it truly counts.

Ultimately, the company's unwavering support showed Alex he was exactly where he needed to be. And for customers looking on, the message was loud and clear: Standing up for inclusivity doesn't have to mean caving to hateful voices; with the right backing and a genuine commitment to DEI, it can become a rallying point that strengthens both brands and communities alike.

As we close this chapter, the stories of Tamela and Alex serve as powerful reminders of the diverse realities DEI practitioners face. Tamela's experience highlighted the risks of entering a workplace unprepared for meaningful dialogue, where the absence of organizational readiness and support undermined both her efforts and her sense of safety. In contrast, Alex's story showed how a prepared, proactive organization can transform a moment of crisis into a reaffirmation of its values, providing safety and validation for those leading the charge.

These narratives converge on a critical truth: Physical and psychological safety in the workplace are nonnegotiable. It is a fundamental right that must be prioritized if DEI efforts are to succeed. While many large organizations have established security protocols and policies, practitioners often need to bring these issues to the forefront. From addressing safety concerns around high-profile initiatives to ensuring thoughtful recognition of cultural and religious holidays, these details are integral to creating environments where everyone feels secure and respected.

Whether you're new to an organization or deeply embedded in its culture, work closely with HR to assess existing policies, identify gaps, and advocate for improvements. Ultimately, all the inclusive policies, campaigns, and workshops in the world mean little if the basic need for safety—both physical and emotional—isn't guaranteed. It is only in secure environments that we can foster true belonging and achieve transformative outcomes.

# CHAPTER 11
## Stories of Safety and Inclusivity

On the following pages we'll explore two distinct narratives—Alicia's and David's—that bring to life the concepts of safety and inclusivity we've been discussing. While their stories unfold in very different ways, each provides a window into the complexities of making workplaces truly equitable and welcoming.

You'll see how Alicia faced an uphill battle in an environment that only gave lip service to inclusion, and how David's efforts took root in an organization ready to invest in real change. Together, these stories shine a light on the resilience required to champion DEI, the courage it takes to stand up for inclusivity, and the emotional toll it can take when the journey isn't supported.

As you read about their challenges and victories, pay attention to the moments that resonate with your own experiences or that offer new insights into your work. Their voices echo a shared desire for a more equitable and secure world—one where safety and inclusivity aren't just ideals, but lived realities.

So let's step into their stories. Let them inspire us to reflect on our own paths, remind us why we do what we do, and energize us to continue pushing forward. Together, these narratives underscore the profound impact DEI efforts can have on individuals, organizations, and the broader community—and they're here to guide us toward action, growth, and a renewed commitment to meaningful change

## ALICIA'S CROSSROADS

Alicia had devoted a decade of her professional life to DEI work, focusing heavily on closing gender gaps in traditionally male-dominated industries. When she joined a midsized manufacturing company, she was optimistic. The organization had publicly committed to becoming more inclusive and diversifying its workforce—a vision that aligned perfectly with Alicia's passion.

## AN AMBITIOUS PROGRAM

After her first few months, Alicia carefully crafted a multiphased initiative designed to attract, retain, and advance women in the company.

- **Recruitment and outreach:** She proposed partnering with technical colleges and women-in-STEM networks, offering internships and scholarships to women interested in manufacturing.
- **Mentorship and training:** She planned small-group workshops, pairing experienced male engineers with female new hires to foster mutual understanding and skill-sharing. A separate mentorship track would provide women with leadership coaching and career development resources.
- **Workplace flexibility:** Recognizing that rigid schedules often deter women juggling family commitments, Alicia suggested more flexible shifts and a robust parental leave policy.

She backed these proposals with detailed research: reports on the business benefits of a gender-balanced workforce, compelling retention statistics, and benchmarking data showing how competitors were gaining market share by embracing DEI initiatives.

## LEADERSHIP'S HESITATION

When Alicia pitched her program to the C-suite, she discovered her optimism wasn't shared. While they gave lip service to supporting DEI, the executives had concerns that ran deeper than she initially realized:

1. **Disruption concerns:** Several executives worried that Alicia's plan would disrupt established routines and shift too many resources into "unproven programs." The plant manager, in particular, believed that "too much change too fast" could spark resentment or confusion among the existing workforce.

2. **Cost and ROI fears:** Even though Alicia's proposal included a modest budget, the CFO was skeptical about the immediate financial return on investing in recruitment, mentorship, and flexible scheduling. They wanted quick, quarterly results—something Alicia's long-term strategy couldn't guarantee.
3. **Cultural resistance:** Beneath the surface, there was an undercurrent of skepticism about whether women could thrive in a rough, physically demanding environment. Some in leadership expressed concern (often couched in "good intentions") that women might find the work unappealing. Alicia tried to explain that the program was about dismantling exactly these assumptions, but her explanations fell on deaf ears.

## FEELING BOXED IN

The lack of organizational support began to weigh heavily on Alicia.

- **Microaggressions and undermining:** In strategy meetings, she was frequently asked to justify the program's "value," even though she had compiled thorough data multiple times. A few key decision-makers would roll their eyes or sigh audibly whenever she brought up the word *equity*.
- **Budget constraints:** A once-promising allocation to fund internal mentorship and outreach programs got slashed to a token amount. Alicia was asked to "prove the concept" with minimal resources. She felt set up to fail before she even began.
- **Emotional toll:** Alicia realized she was spending more time defending the *idea* of diversity than actually *implementing* it. She worked long hours, taking her frustration home each evening. Eventually, the stress began affecting her health and her passion for the work.

## A TIPPING POINT

After multiple attempts to get her initiative off the ground, Alicia faced the harsh truth: The leadership team cared more about preserving the status quo than fostering genuine change. They might have "believed in DEI" in theory, but not enough to reshape old processes or risk short-term profit dips.

She held one final meeting with the C-suite, laying out the long-term gains of a balanced workforce: higher retention, innovation boosts from diverse perspectives, and positive employer branding. Despite her thorough presentation, the response was lukewarm at best, dismissive at worst.

## CHOOSING HERSELF

Back at her desk, surrounded by program notes and spreadsheets, Alicia took a long breath. She realized her commitment to DEI was unshakable, but her belief in *this* particular company's readiness was now gone. The repeated resistance had not only derailed her program but also eroded her well-being and sense of professional integrity.

- **Self-preservation:** Alicia recognized she deserved an environment that valued her expertise and the communities she aimed to serve.
- **Integrity over comfort:** Walking away meant leaving a stable paycheck, but staying felt like she was betraying her own commitment to real inclusion.

After careful reflection—and some late-night conversations with trusted mentors—she decided to resign. In her exit interview, she was clear but respectful: The work she came to do wasn't possible if leadership wasn't genuinely invested.

## A FORWARD STEP

Alicia's departure was more than an act of self-care; it was a statement about the seriousness of DEI work. She would rather bring her decade of expertise to a place that truly understood the value of a diverse, empowered workforce. Though leaving felt bittersweet, Alicia walked away with her principles intact and her future wide open.

In the aftermath, she took time off to recover from the stress and recalibrate her goals. Doors soon opened at another organization that not only welcomed her program ideas but actively sought them out. For Alicia, moving on wasn't just a move toward self-preservation—it was a necessary step in honoring the integrity and impact she'd spent her career cultivating.

## DAVID'S VICTORY FOR INCLUSIVITY

David had been a DEI officer at his organization for just over a year when a transgender employee approached him with a concern: the lack of inclusive bathroom facilities. This employee felt anxiety and discomfort every time this person needed to use the restroom and wasn't alone. David recognized immediately that this was more than an isolated issue—it was an opportunity to foster a more equitable workplace.

## OPPORTUNITY FOR CHANGE

When David heard about the employee's experience, his immediate thought was, *This can't wait.* He knew that small gestures of inclusivity—like accessible, gender-neutral bathrooms—often carry an outsized impact on employees' overall sense of belonging.

- **Initial discovery:** David learned there were no private, all-gender restrooms on-site. Employees had to use either men's or women's facilities, which could lead to discomfort—or

even harassment—for those who did not identify with those categories.
- **Employee impact:** Several staff members (including allies) had quietly expressed similar concerns to HR in the past, but the issue had never made it to the top of the priority list.

## ORGANIZATIONAL READINESS AND LEADERSHIP SUPPORT

Unlike some workplaces resistant to DEI initiatives, David's organization had laid groundwork over the years that signaled *they might be ready for change*:

- **Previous commitments:** The company had already implemented LGBTQ+ sensitivity training, published inclusive hiring statements, and participated in Pride-related community events.
- **Open-door leadership:** Key C-suite executives had encouraged employees to raise concerns and pitch ideas for improvement. They saw DEI not just as a checkbox but as a potential driver of innovation and positive morale.
- **HR partnership:** The HR department was eager to collaborate. They recognized that inclusive bathrooms were a missing puzzle piece in the company's broader DEI strategy.

## BUILDING THE PILOT PROGRAM

David got to work creating a proposal for a pilot program. His plan included

- **Converting existing spaces:** Identifying one or two single-stall restrooms that could be quickly repurposed as gender-neutral, complete with updated signage and locks for privacy.

- **Gathering data and feedback:** Working with HR to distribute a short survey assessing employee comfort levels and willingness to use all-gender restrooms. David also planned to conduct small focus groups in which employees could discuss any concerns.
- **Establishing a budget:** The changes weren't expensive—new signage and some minor renovations—but David documented every cost to reassure leadership that this was a worthwhile, manageable investment.
- **Outlining a communication strategy:** Crafting email announcements, intranet updates, and a succinct FAQ explaining what the gender-neutral restrooms were, why they mattered, and how to address common questions or misconceptions.

## PRESENTING THE CASE

David pitched his plan to a cross-functional team that included members of the C-suite, facilities management, and HR. Drawing on data from other companies that had successfully rolled out all-gender restrooms, he emphasized the tangible benefits:

- **Employee well-being:** Reduced anxiety for transgender, non-binary, and gender-nonconforming employees.
- **Talent retention and attraction:** Demonstrating a commitment to inclusion could help in recruiting (and keeping) top talent.
- **Company culture:** Fostering a sense of belonging often correlates with higher engagement, productivity, and overall job satisfaction.

## LEADERSHIP'S RESPONSE

To David's relief, the response was overwhelmingly positive:

- **Enthusiasm at the top:** A senior VP thanked David for highlighting an issue they had "honestly never considered in depth."

He acknowledged his own learning curve around gender identity and expressed excitement about "leading the way" in the industry.
- **Immediate green light:** The CFO—initially concerned about budget—found David's cost estimates reasonable. By calling it a pilot program, David made it clear the changes were measured and scalable.
- **Unified support:** HR offered to set up an internal communications campaign, while facilities management quickly identified restrooms that could be converted. The CEO even mentioned the initiative in a company-wide town hall, praising the shift toward a more inclusive culture.

## IMPLEMENTING THE CHANGES

Once given the green light, David and his team moved swiftly:

1. **Signage and renovations:** Within a few weeks, the designated restrooms featured new all-gender restroom signs, along with locks ensuring privacy.
2. **Training and awareness:** HR rolled out a mini-training session for managers on how to address potential questions or pushback. They also provided talking points for team leads.
3. **Feedback loops:** Employees were encouraged to use an anonymous form to share their experiences—good, bad, or indifferent. David and HR checked this feedback regularly and adjusted signage or accessibility features as needed.

## EMPLOYEE REACTION

The transgender employee who initially approached David was relieved and grateful to see actionable steps taken so quickly. They felt their concerns were heard and validated—an experience far too rare in many workplaces. Other employees, including cisgender individuals, expressed appreciation for having more restroom options, praising the company for its responsiveness.

## BEYOND BATHROOMS: A NEW LENS ON POLICY

Bolstered by the success of the pilot, the company decided to take a more expansive look at its policies and practices:

- **Name and pronoun guidelines:** They reviewed forms, email signature templates, and ID badges to ensure employees could display their correct names and pronouns.
- **Dress code flexibility:** They updated the dress code to be more gender-neutral and reflective of the varied needs in manufacturing environments.
- **Ongoing culture building:** Management began a broader conversation on allyship and how to support employees across the spectrum of identities.

## REFLECTION

For David, this project stood out as a clear victory—a testament to how *organizational readiness* and *one act of advocacy* can unlock broader change. Here's what he learned:

- **Readiness matters:** Had leadership been resistant, the outcome might have been drastically different. In this case, the organization's prior commitments to DEI laid the groundwork for a smooth rollout.
- **Collaboration is key:** By partnering with HR, facilities, and executive sponsors, David demonstrated that DEI isn't just an "HR issue"—it's integrated into all aspects of a business.

- **Visibility and validation:** Addressing a specific, concrete need—like gender-neutral bathrooms—can spark deeper cultural shifts. Sometimes, one tangible success propels an organization to tackle more systemic issues.

## A BEACON OF INCLUSIVITY

David's swift and empathetic response not only addressed the transgender employee's immediate concern but also ignited a company-wide review of policies through a new inclusivity lens. His story is a powerful reminder that when *one employee's voice* is met with *true organizational readiness*, the ripple effects can foster a safer, more respectful workplace for all.

I shared Alicia's and David's stories to show how DEI work can play out in completely different ways—yet both paths offer lessons on resilience, integrity, and the power of community. Maybe you've found yourself in situations like Alicia's, where leadership's support was all talk and no action, leaving you drained and doubting your own impact. Or perhaps you've had moments like David's, where one small step opened the door to bigger, lasting change.

Either way, these stories highlight the importance of recognizing whether your environment genuinely embraces DEI or merely tolerates it. They also underscore the role of safety—both emotional and professional—in making real progress. It's a coalition effort: when you find like-minded allies who value inclusivity, you create a space where people can speak up, push boundaries, and truly thrive.

So if you see parallels to your own journey, let these narratives serve as both validation and inspiration. Whether you're fighting an uphill battle or riding the wave of supportive leadership, remember that you're not alone. Continue showing up, trusting your instincts, and protecting your well-being. Know when it's time to dig deeper—and when it's time to step away. In either case, your commitment to equity remains the driving force that can shift cultures, one brave act at a time. Here are a few questions to ask yourself when assessing your safety.

## REFLECTIVE QUESTIONS

1. Where do I see gaps between stated support for DEI and real, tangible action in my own work environment?
2. How can I prioritize my emotional and professional well-being, even when I'm deeply invested in driving change?
3. What small but impactful steps can I take—or celebrate—in moving my organization toward genuine inclusivity?

# CHAPTER 12
## Conflict Resolution and Resilience

All right, folks, let's dive into a topic that's as essential as a good cup of coffee on a Monday morning: conflict resolution and resilience. Here's the scoop: conflict is like an uninvited guest at your dinner party—it shows up, and it's up to you to manage it.

Picture this: You're steering the DEI ship in your organization, working hard to foster inclusion and equity. Suddenly—bam!—conflict arises. Maybe it's a heated debate during a diversity training session or a disagreement over a new policy. Conflict can rear its head in various forms, from misunderstandings to full-blown disputes.

So why does this matter for us? Because conflict is like that unexpected plot twist in a movie—it keeps us on our toes. We're not just the champions of diversity; we're also the peacemakers, the bridge builders, and the go-to problem solvers. Conflict is part and parcel of our gig, and how we handle it can make or break our efforts.

But what about resilience? Well, friend, resilience is our secret weapon. It's like the superhero cape we wear when things get tough. When we're dealing with sensitive issues, resistance, and sometimes overwhelming trauma, resilience is our lifeline.

Think about it. We're constantly navigating through challenging terrain, tackling biases, and advocating for historically excluded communities. It's not all rainbows and butterflies; it can get downright tough. That's where resilience comes in. It gives us the ability to bounce back, to keep fighting, even when the odds seem stacked against us. And it allows us to help others do the same.

Our organizations and the people we work with depend on us to guide them through rough waters. They look to us for solutions, for that steady hand when things get rocky. That's why understanding conflict resolution and having resilience in our toolkit is so darn important.

So get ready to roll up your sleeves and dive into the world of conflict resolution and resilience. We're going to explore the skills, tools, and strategies that help you not only survive but thrive in this work. It's a wild ride, but together, we've got this!

## HANDLING CONFLICT CONSTRUCTIVELY

For seasoned practitioners, the path is already well trodden. You've been through the trenches, facilitated countless discussions, and championed the cause of diversity and inclusion in myriad other ways. Yet conflicts will continue to arise, sometimes as familiar guests and other times as unexpected visitors.

But conflict isn't a hindrance; it's a pivot point for growth and change. It's a reminder that the work you do is challenging yet invaluable. It's a testament to the progress you've made, but also a signal that there's more to be done.

So take a moment to acknowledge your strength and commitment. You've weathered storms and celebrated victories. Your work has made a difference in the lives of many, and that's worth celebrating. When conflicts arise, remember that you're not alone; you have a community of fellow practitioners and allies standing beside you. And as a seasoned practitioner, you may already have your own strategies for handling conflicts. But it's always helpful to have a structured framework to reference, so I offer you mine:

## CONFLICT RESOLUTION FRAMEWORK

- **Identify and define the issue:** Start by ensuring that the central issue is well-defined and understood by all parties involved.
- **Create a safe space:** Reiterate the importance of a safe and inclusive environment. Remind participants of ground rules that encourage respect and active listening.
- **Explore needs:** Encourage individuals to delve into their underlying interests and unmet needs. This often uncovers the root causes of conflicts.
- **Generate options:** Facilitate creative brainstorming to explore potential solutions. Seasoned practitioners often find innovative ways to address conflicts.

- **Evaluate and select solutions:** Objectively assess options for feasibility, impact, and alignment with your objective principles. Choose the solution(s) that best address the core issues.
- **Agree on an action plan:** Develop a clear action plan with specific steps, assigned responsibilities, timelines, and milestones.
- **Follow up and reflect:** Implement the action plan and schedule follow-up sessions to monitor progress. Reflect on the conflict resolution process and continue to learn and refine your approach.

Remember, conflict doesn't mean you're failing in your efforts; it means you're challenging the status quo and pushing for positive change. With your experience and this framework, conflicts can become opportunities to deepen understanding, foster inclusion, and advance equity. You've got this!

## RESILIENCE IN CHALLENGING TIMES

My journey as a practitioner has been both rewarding and challenging. It often feels like an unending battle in which I celebrate victories but also face discouraging setbacks. I've witnessed the war on DEI work, with some companies that once proudly championed diversity and inclusion taking steps backward. Pressured by various factors, they've cut funding, reduced other resources, or even abandoned their diversity commitments altogether. These actions have been disheartening, especially when I've dedicated myself to advancing the cause. However, resilience has become my armor; it's what keeps me moving forward even in the face of adversity.

Resilience is not just about bouncing back. It's about pushing forward, even when the terrain gets tough. It's the ability to withstand setbacks, adapt to change, and maintain a sense of purpose and well-being in the face of challenges.

## BUILDING AND SUSTAINING RESILIENCE

Maintaining resilience requires a deliberate approach. Here are some effective strategies that I've found:

- **Stay connected:** I reach out to my community. Sharing my experiences, listening to others' stories, and drawing strength from collective wisdom has been invaluable. Networks of like-minded individuals have provided me with support and encouragement during challenging times.
- **Focus on the bigger picture:** When faced with setbacks, I remind myself of the greater purpose. DEI work isn't just about my organization; it's about the broader societal change I'm contributing to. Keeping this perspective has renewed my sense of purpose.
- **Self-care:** I've recognized that the battle for diversity and inclusion can be emotionally taxing. Prioritizing self-care, whether it's through mindfulness, exercise, or support from mental health professionals, has been crucial. I've also set boundaries to ensure a balance between my work and my personal lives.
- **Adaptability:** Resilience is closely tied to adaptability. As the DEI landscape evolves, I've remained open to adjusting my strategies. Flexibility has allowed me to navigate changing circumstances effectively.
- **Learn from setbacks:** I've viewed every setback as an opportunity for growth and learning. Analyzing what went wrong and how I can apply those lessons to future endeavors has been essential. I've understood that even setbacks are steps forward in the journey.
- **Advocacy and allies:** Seeking allies within and outside my organization who can champion DEI alongside me has been impactful. Together, we've amplified our impact and navigated challenges as a team. Building a support network of allies has strengthened my resilience.

## EXAMPLES OF BUILDING RESILIENCE

- **Maya's community support:** Maya, a DEI manager, faced a setback when her organization halted a diversity program she had worked tirelessly to develop. In response, she reached out to her networks and found a supportive community of practitioners who offered guidance and encouragement. Together, they organized webinars and discussions, which not only rekindled her motivation but also expanded her knowledge and her support network.
- **John's adaptability:** John had been leading DEI efforts in his company for years when new leadership rolled back key diversity initiatives. Rather than becoming discouraged, John adapted his approach. He began focusing on grassroots efforts, engaging employees at all levels, and raising awareness about the importance of DEI. Over time his persistence paid off, and the organization renewed its commitment.

Building and sustaining resilience is an ongoing journey. In the fight for diversity and inclusion, resilience is our shield against setbacks and fuel for progress. By staying connected, maintaining a sense of purpose, prioritizing self-care, enforcing personal boundaries, and learning from setbacks, we can continue to champion DEI even in the face of adversity. The battle may be challenging, but our resilience will help us continue to drive positive change.

# CHAPTER 13
## Leading with Inclusive Excellence

As practitioners, our journey is unique. We must step up as the leaders many of us never had. Leadership has shifted from the traditional top-down model to one of approachability and support. People no longer settle for leaders who just issue commands; they seek leaders who listen, coach, empathize, and collaborate actively. Inclusivity has become a foundation of this transformation. We're not just leaders; we are trailblazers, catalysts for change, and champions of equity. In this chapter, I'll keep it concise and dive into a transformative exploration of what it means to be a truly inclusive leader, particularly for those of us in this field.

## LEADING BY EXAMPLE

At the core of our roles as practitioners lies a profound responsibility to lead by example. We must be unwavering role models of inclusivity and equity in every aspect of our work and lives. So as we delve deeper into the intricacies of inclusive leadership, we will discuss the values that underpin it and provide practical strategies that can empower you to be the change agents your organizations and communities need.

In the chapters that follow, we'll share insights, real-life stories, and actionable steps to help you become an even more effective and influential practitioner. My mission is not just to articulate these concepts but to equip you to apply them as role models who make a tangible difference in the lives of those you serve.

## KNOWING OURSELVES AND OTHERS

Inclusive leadership begins with a deep self-awareness, especially concerning our own biases and privileges. We must understand our own unique perspectives and experiences to connect authentically with others. In short, the journey toward inclusion starts with us.

- **Think like a game changer:** We must think beyond immediate challenges and obstacles to envision a world in which *diversity* and *equity* are not just buzzwords but lived realities. Our visionary thinking should inspire our teams and organizations to embrace these ideals.
- **Take action and keep it real:** Inclusivity is not a passive concept; it demands intentional and principled action. Our decisions and actions should reflect our commitment to fairness, justice, and equity. When integrity is the cornerstone of our work, we can create a culture of trust and accountability.
- **Coaching and guidance:** In the evolving leadership landscape, individuals are increasingly seeking coaching and guidance from leaders. Consider a scenario in which a young professional, passionate about diversity and inclusion, seeks mentorship from an experienced practitioner. The mentor offers valuable insights, helping the mentee navigate the complexities of fostering inclusivity in their own sphere of influence.

I firmly believe that to be successful as a leader, one must possess all these attributes of inclusive leadership. There's no longer room for leadership that is devoid of awareness, vision, or integrity. Our journey as practitioners is a continuous evolution. By leading with our core values, we have the power to shape a more equitable future for all. Remember, we are not only leaders but torchbearers of change. The world is watching!

## FOSTERING INCLUSIVITY

Working in this space, we totally get how crucial it is to have a diverse team. But let's be real: Sometimes we end up with squads that look a lot like us. Here's the scoop on how to face this challenge and build teams that truly celebrate diversity while keeping inclusivity on point:

- **Make diversity your MVP:** Diversity isn't just a buzzword; it's the MVP of your team-building game. It's time to go all in on this strategy. Actively seek out individuals from different walks of life, backgrounds, and experiences. When your team offers an assortment of perspectives, you're setting the stage for game-changing innovation and creativity.

- **Inclusivity is the ultimate team bond:** Diversity is a great start, but inclusivity is what glues your team together. Create an atmosphere where every team member feels like a rock star. Encourage open lines of communication, be a boss at listening, and make sure respect rules the roost. When your crew knows their voices matter, that's when the real team magic happens.
- **Take on bias and stereotypes like a champ:** Let's face it; we all carry some biases and stereotypes in our backpacks. It's time to unpack that stuff. Challenge those biases within yourself and within your organization. When you're putting together your dream team, use some slick techniques like blind hiring and get a diverse crew in on those interviews. This way you're leveling the playing field and making sure bias doesn't call the shots.

And here's the kicker: When your organization sees how successful you are at building a diverse team, your strategy can become the blueprint for other leaders and departments. You'll be leading the charge in creating a more inclusive workplace for everyone.

To wrap it up, as practitioners, we've got to be on point when it comes to building teams that rep the diversity we're all about. Putting diversity front and center, rocking inclusivity, and tackling subconscious bias are the moves that'll help us assemble the ultimate dream team and inspire others to follow suit, bringing meaningful change to the table.

# CHAPTER 14
## Allies and Advocacy

In the ever-evolving landscape of diversity, equity, and inclusion, one term that continues to gain prominence is *allyship*. Becoming an ally involves more than adopting a title or a label; it is a commitment on a journey toward creating a more equitable and inclusive world. Allies play a pivotal role in amplifying the voices of historically excluded communities, standing up against injustice, and working toward a society where everyone is heard, valued, and treated with dignity.

As practitioners, we often find ourselves in the role of allies. We become the voice for those who have been left out of the conversation, advocating for their rights, needs, and perspectives. Our role extends beyond lip service; it requires a commitment to dismantling systemic biases and working tirelessly to create inclusive environments where all individuals can thrive.

Before we delve into the stories of practitioners who have embraced their roles as allies, I'd like to share my perspective on what it means to be an ally.

## EMBRACING THE JOURNEY OF ALLYSHIP

My journey toward becoming an ally has been an integral part of my professional and personal growth. I've come to understand that being an ally is not just a role I play within my organization; it's a fundamental aspect of my identity and purpose.

## SELF-EDUCATION

My commitment to allyship starts with self-education. I recognize that to be an effective ally, I must continually educate myself about the systemic injustices faced by historically excluded communities. It's not enough to have a superficial understanding; I delve deep into the origins of discrimination, the intricacies of intersectionality, and the lived experiences of those who have been historically excluded. This education empowers me to advocate more effectively.

## ACTIVE LISTENING

In my role, I've learned the immense value of active listening. Creating spaces for open and honest dialogue is crucial. I sit down with employees from diverse backgrounds and listen to their stories, challenges, and aspirations. I've found that by actively hearing their voices, I can better understand the specific needs and concerns they face.

## AMPLIFICATION, NOT APPROPRIATION

It's essential to recognize that, even using active listening, I can never fully understand the lived experiences of all historically excluded individuals. Therefore, my role is not to speak for them but to use my privilege and platform to amplify their own voices. I work diligently to ensure that their stories and perspectives are at the forefront of the initiatives I champion.

## CHALLENGING BIASES

Part of my responsibility is to challenge biases, my own and those within my organization. I'm not afraid to confront microaggressions or address stereotypes, even when it's uncomfortable. I firmly believe that challenging these biases is a crucial step toward creating a more inclusive workplace.

## TAKING ACTION

Allyship is not passive; it's about taking action. In my role, I actively support historically excluded communities by advocating for policy changes, designing and facilitating educational programs, and participating in community engagement initiatives. I use my position to influence positive change within my organization and beyond.

## A PERSONAL COMMITMENT TO ALLYSHIP

Before we dive into the stories, I want to reflect on the importance of connection and why I am so deeply committed to this work. In my own journey, I dedicate my time and energy to this work despite the struggles I face—like any human, I am constantly navigating biases of my own. I don't get it right all the time. But I remain committed to learning, creating safe spaces, and holding myself accountable.

This commitment has drawn me closer to my faith and strengthened my walk as a woman of Christ. At the heart of my faith is love, and I try hard to approach each situation with as much love and curiosity as I can. When I make mistakes, I give myself grace and mercy, because I know that growth requires self-compassion.

> *"But grow in the grace and knowledge of our Lord and Savior Jesus Christ. To him be glory both now and forever! Amen."* — **2 Peter 3:18**

As a DEI practitioner, my role as an ally is a deeply personal calling. Every initiative I design—whether fostering understanding, advocating for inclusive policies, or creating safe spaces for dialogue—stems from this commitment. I am intentional about measuring progress with data and forging partnerships with organizations that amplify our collective impact.

This work isn't just a job—it's a mission to be a catalyst for meaningful change, to uplift historically excluded voices, and to evolve continuously toward a more inclusive world. Allyship is not just theoretical for us; it's an ongoing practice woven into the fabric of who we are as practitioners.

With this in mind, let's explore the stories of three DEI practitioners—Maria, Raj, and Jamal—and how they've embraced their roles as allies, creating ripple effects of change in their communities.

## FOSTERING INCLUSIVE SPACES—
## MARIA'S INFLUENCE

Maria, a DEI director, is known for her unwavering commitment to fostering inclusive spaces within her organization. But Maria's drive for accessibility wasn't just about compliance—it was rooted in empathy born from witnessing a close friend's struggle with physical limitations in public spaces. She understood the isolation that comes when environments are built without everyone in mind.

Recognizing the absence of accommodations for individuals with disabilities, Maria launched a comprehensive accessibility initiative. She advocated for the redesign of office spaces to be physically accessible, introduced assistive technologies for meetings, and implemented staff training to ensure colleagues knew how to support those with disabilities meaningfully.

The ripple effect of Maria's allyship was profound. Conversations about accessibility transformed from being logistical concerns to matters of dignity and belonging. Colleagues began embracing the values of accessibility, making it a core part of the company's culture. Maria's dedication expanded the organization's understanding of what it means to be inclusive, inspiring others to lead with empathy and action.

## CHAMPIONING LGBTQ+ INCLUSION—
## RAJ'S ADVOCACY

Raj, a passionate DEI coordinator and a member of the LGBTQ+ community, believes that the source of allyship should extend beyond those with shared identities—it's about fostering solidarity and understanding among people with different life experiences too. His passion for advocacy stemmed from personal experiences of navigating spaces where he often felt invisible and misunderstood. Raj knew firsthand the healing power of support and community.

Determined to make a difference, Raj spearheaded initiatives to create safe spaces and resources for LGBTQ+ employees. But he didn't stop there. He recognized the powerful work of allies in creating sustainable change. Raj organized listening sessions during which LGBTQ+ employees shared their stories and allies could learn firsthand about those experiences.

Over time, the ripple effect of Raj's work became evident. Empowered by his leadership, allies stepped up to organize Pride Month events, initiated diversity training, and championed LGBTQ+-inclusive policies. Raj's advocacy didn't just foster inclusion—it nurtured a culture of understanding and courage, where allyship became a shared responsibility.

## PROMOTING RACIAL EQUITY– JAMAL'S LEADERSHIP

Jamal, a DEI manager, is deeply committed to promoting racial equity. His commitment was shaped by his own experiences as a person of color navigating professional spaces that often felt isolating. Jamal knew that true allyship required not just awareness but intentional, sustained action.

With this understanding, Jamal led efforts to address systemic biases within the organization. He advocated for equity-focused policies, racial sensitivity training, and diverse hiring practices. But Jamal didn't view himself as the sole driver of change—he believed in empowering allies to use their privilege to amplify historically excluded voices.

The ripple effect of Jamal's leadership was transformational. Allies began to challenge systemic biases openly, advocate for inclusive hiring, and support their colleagues in meaningful ways. Over time, the organization underwent a cultural shift—it didn't just become more diverse but also more committed to equity and justice.

## CHAMPIONING HISTORICALLY EXCLUDED VOICES

As DEI practitioners, we know that one of our most profound responsibilities is the intentional and unwavering support of historically excluded voices. This is not just a moral obligation—it is the very foundation of our work. We bear the responsibility of ensuring that those who have been silenced, overlooked, or denied access to opportunity are not only heard but valued. This commitment extends beyond our job titles or organizational initiatives; it is a calling to cocreate a world that is truly equitable and inclusive.

Many of us in this work come from historically excluded communities ourselves. We do not just advocate for change; we live the realities of exclusion, often navigating the intersection of lived experience and institutional responsibility. We carry the weight of pushing for systems transformation while ensuring our own belonging within spaces that were not designed with us in mind. This dual role makes our work deeply personal and uniquely powerful.

Yet we also know that supporting historically excluded voices is not a passive act; it is a sustained, intentional commitment that requires vigilance, humility, and a refusal to accept the status quo. It means dismantling systemic barriers, challenging hidden biases, and creating tangible pathways for those who have been marginalized to lead, thrive, and shape the future.

## CHALLENGES

- **Systemic barriers:** We see how deeply entrenched systemic inequities shape the experiences of historically excluded individuals. Exclusionary policies, inequitable access to resources, and the absence of representation in leadership are not accidental; they are symptoms of structures built to maintain power and privilege.

- **For example:** When leadership teams lack racial, gender, or neurodivergent diversity, we know that the policies and decision-making structures will reflect those same gaps, reinforcing cycles of exclusion.
- **Subconscious bias:** Even in organizations committed to change, we continue to witness the ways implicit biases shape hiring, promotions, and everyday interactions. These biases—often unexamined—create environments where individuals from historically excluded backgrounds are underestimated, undervalued, or overlooked.
  - **For example:** A manager may unintentionally gravitate toward employees who mirror his or her own cultural background or communication style, limiting opportunities for those who bring different perspectives to the table.

## OPPORTUNITIES

- **The power of representation:** We know that representation at the highest levels is not just symbolic—it is transformational. When historically excluded individuals are in positions of power, they do more than fill a seat; they shift culture, redefine leadership, and open doors for others to follow.
  - **For example:** A CEO from a historically excluded background doesn't just diversify leadership; they signal to employees that inclusion is not performative but embedded in the organization's DNA.
- **Education as a catalyst for change:** We understand the power of education in shifting mindsets and disrupting harmful norms. When organizations commit to ongoing learning—through structured dialogues, policy evaluations, and training—they equip their people with the tools to recognize and challenge inequities.
  - **or example:** A workshop on *intersectional leadership* can help decision-makers understand how overlapping

identities—such as race, gender, disability, and socioeconomic background—impact workplace experiences. By applying an intersectional lens, organizations can move beyond one-size-fits-all approaches to create truly inclusive policies and cultures.

## STRATEGIES FOR SUSTAINABLE CHANGE

- **Creating safe and empowering spaces:** We know that inclusion is not about asking people to assimilate—it is about making space for authenticity. Whether through affinity groups, psychological safety initiatives, or open forums, we must ensure that historically excluded voices have platforms to be heard and influence change.
  - **For example:** Regular diversity dialogues where employees can share their lived experiences foster a culture of trust, accountability, and collective learning.
- **Mentorship and sponsorship:** Access to networks, advocacy, and career sponsorship is critical for professional advancement. As practitioners, we continue to push for mentorship and sponsorship programs that do more than advise—they create opportunities.
  - **For example:** When senior leaders not only mentor but actively champion and open doors for employees from underrepresented backgrounds, they disrupt the exclusionary patterns that have long dictated who rises and who remains unseen.

Historically excluded voices do more than bring diversity into an organization. They spark innovation, challenge outdated systems, and expand our collective understanding of what is possible. Our work is not about surface-level inclusion; it is about fundamentally reshaping the structures that dictate who belongs, who leads, and who thrives.

This is why we remain steadfast. Because diversity, equity, inclusion, and accessibility are not abstract ideals—they are the blueprints for a better world. And as practitioners, we do not just advocate for this future—we build it, brick by brick.

So let's keep pushing. Let's keep creating space for every voice to be heard, valued, and uplifted. Because at the end of the day, our legacy will not be measured by the words we say but by the lives we impact and the change we make real.

# CHAPTER 15

## Core Values

Core values are the ingrained principles and convictions that anchor our actions and attitudes and form the blueprint for our advocacy. As DEI practitioners, we transcend compliance and surface engagement. Our mission demands a profound commitment to core values that guide both our professional and personal ethics.

This chapter delves into core values and the intrinsic role they play. We will explore their significance as the foundation of trust, consistency, and reputation. And we will reflect on how these values shape our identity, reinforce our commitment, and influence our capacity to effect meaningful change within human diversity's multilayered tapestry.

## **IDENTIFYING CORE VALUES**

Personal core values are the principles that define our ethics and guide our behavior. They are influenced by culture, family, experiences, and education, and they direct our decisions, beliefs, and interactions.

Identifying personal core values is a journey of introspection. It's about pinpointing what drives us, what we are passionate about, and which principles we hold sacred. This is accomplished by engaging in self-reflection: identify moments of happiness, pride, or fulfillment and consider the values behind them. To recognize when our values were compromised, reflect on times of disappointment. Consider which values are nonnegotiable and which have been challenged or pressed upon. Understand which values are celebrated or diminished within you during moments of excitement or frustration.

It is critical to ensure we possess great clarity of our core values, as they are essential to our growth as leaders and practitioners. To that end, I designed the following core values assessment as a deep dive into discovering yours.

## CORE VALUES ASSESSMENT

### List of Core Values

- Authenticity
- Wisdom
- Resilience
- Altruism
- Empowerment
- Balance
- Diversity
- Flexibility
- Accountability
- Curiosity
- Adaptability
- Optimism
- Mindfulness
- Teamwork
- Courage
- Simplicity
- Gratitude
- Resourcefulness
- Honesty
- Innovation
- Sustainability
- Adventure
- Self-expression
- Harmony
- Creativity
- Fairness
- Trust
- Serenity
- Patience
- Humility
- Open-mindedness
- Ambition
- Kindness
- Freedom
- Connection
- Spirituality
- Justice
- Family
- Self-compassion
- Purpose
- Generosity
- Empathy
- Integrity
- Independence
- Love
- Health and well-being
- Community
- Personal growth
- Tolerance
- Fun
- Achievement
- Boldness
- Challenge
- Faith
- Happiness
- Humor
- Inclusiveness
- Knowledge
- Leadership
- Learning

- Loyalty
- Passion
- Professionalism
- Quality
- Respect
- Responsibility
- Security
- Service
- Stability
- Success
- Teamwork
- Wellness
- Aliveness
- Benevolence
- Openness
- Transparency
- Unity
- Zest
- Stewardship

**Activity:** Identify your top ten core values and narrow to your top five.

**Objective:** Identifying and prioritizing your top ten core values and then narrowing them down to your top five most essential values will assist you in gaining clarity about what truly matters to you in life.

**Materials Needed:** A pen and paper or a digital note-taking device.

**Instructions**

**Step 1: Generate your list (ten minutes)**

> Find a quiet and comfortable space where you can focus without distractions.
> Take out your pen and paper or open a digital note-taking application.
> Review the comprehensive list of core values provided above.
> Without overthinking, jot down any core values that resonate with you as you read through the list. Write down as many as you'd like. This step is about initial exploration, so don't worry about the number; the goal is to capture what comes to mind naturally.

### Step 2: Reflect (ten minutes)

- ➤ Review the list of core values you've written down.
- ➤ Reflect on each value and consider why it's important to you. Ask yourself questions like, "What does this value mean to me?" or "How does this value manifest in my life?"

### Step 3: Prioritize (fifteen minutes)

- ➤ Begin by ranking your list of core values from one to ten, with one being the most important and ten being the least important. Take your time to compare each value and its significance to you. Make adjustments as needed.
- ➤ Once you've ranked them, review your top-ten values and ensure you're comfortable with your rankings.

### Step 4: Narrow to top five (ten minutes)

- ➤ Now it's time to narrow your list down further. Choose your top five values from the list of ten you've just ranked. This step may require some difficult decisions, but focus on the values that truly define who you are and that guide your actions and decisions.

### Step 5: Assess (fifteen minutes)

- ➤ Reflect on each of your top five core values using the reflection questions below.
- ➤ Write a brief paragraph explaining why each of these values is crucial to you.
- ➤ Consider how aligning your life with these values has positively impacted your decisions and actions.
- ➤ Think about any areas in your life where you may want to make adjustments to better live in accordance with your top five core values.

- Consider sharing your top five core values with someone you trust, like a friend or family member, and discuss how these values resonate with you. This can help keep you accountable when you start to waiver in the face of opposition.
- Keep this worksheet accessible and use it to guide your daily decisions and actions.

Core Value 1

Value: _____

Why is this value important to you?

How have you lived by this value in the past?

How can you live by this value more in the future?

Role model who embodies this value and how:

Core Value 2

Value: _____

Why is this value important to you?

How have you lived by this value in the past?

How can you live by this value more in the future?

Role model who embodies this value and how:

Core Value 3

Value: _____

Why is this value important to you?

How have you lived by this value in the past?

How can you live by this value more in the future?

Role model who embodies this value and how:

Core Value 4

Value: _____

Why is this value important to you?

How have you lived by this value in the past?

How can you live by this value more in the future?

Role model who embodies this value and how:

Core Value 5

Value: _____

Why is this value important to you?

How have you lived by this value in the past?

How can you live by this value more in the future?

Role model who embodies this value and how:

Identifying and prioritizing your top five core values is an essential step in personal growth and self-awareness. The following examples illustrate how our values serve as a compass for our life choices and help us live a more fulfilling and purpose-driven life.

- **Inclusive integrity** embraces honesty and transparency, incorporating diverse perspectives and experiences.
- **Equitable excellence** aims for outstanding outcomes through fair processes that allow everyone to reach their potential.
- **Respectful inclusivity** recognizes and values each individual, fostering a sense of belonging.
- **Responsible advocacy** owns the impact of actions and uses influence to promote equity and dismantle barriers.
- **Innovative solidarity** commits to creative, collaborative approaches that advance underrepresented groups.

As change agents, most of us embody these core values in our strategies, advocacy, and interactions, making abstract concepts tangible outcomes that define success. Regularly revisiting and reassessing your core values can help you adapt to changing circumstances and continue to grow.

## LIVING AND UPHOLDING CORE VALUES

On our journey as practitioners, understanding our core values is just the beginning. The real challenge lies in living and upholding these values, especially when faced with situations that test our beliefs. In a role where friction and conflict often arise, it's crucial to have the resilience and strategies to not only maintain but champion our core values.

Next we will explore practical tools and reflective questions that can help us navigate the complexities of upholding our values in any organizational or community context. It's about making our core values our moral compass, driving us to create the change we desire within ourselves, our workplaces, and our communities.

## THE REAL-WORLD CHALLENGE

Actually living by our core values isn't always straightforward, especially in a professional setting. We may encounter situations where our values clash with others' or with organizational policies. This friction can cause discomfort and lead us to question our beliefs. However, it's in these moments that our core values become most crucial. They act as a beacon, guiding us through the fog of uncertainty and conflict. To address these challenges, I employ specific strategies that help me uphold my values.

> **Reflect:** Regularly take time to reflect on your actions and decisions. Ask yourself, "Are my choices aligned with my core values?" This introspection helps you stay true to your beliefs.

**Seek support:** When in doubt, reach out to mentors or colleagues who share similar values. They can provide perspective and advice on how they might navigate challenging situations.

**Educate and advocate:** Use opportunities to educate others about your values and why they are important to you. Advocacy can also mean pushing for changes in policies or practices that contradict your core values.

**Stay informed:** Keeping abreast of the latest developments in DEI can help you stay prepared to better articulate and defend your values in heated or unexpected moments.

## QUESTIONS TO ASK WHEN VALUES ARE CHALLENGED

When you sense a conflict with your values, ask yourself the following questions to gain clarity about how you should proceed:

- **What exactly is causing the conflict?** Identify the specific issue or behavior that is at odds with your values.
- **Why does this conflict with my values?** Understand the root of the discomfort. Is it a matter of ethics, fairness, respect, or something else?
- **What can I do to resolve this conflict in a way that upholds my values?** Consider actions that can help align the situation more closely with your beliefs.
- **Who can I consult for guidance or support?** Sometimes discussing the issue with a trusted individual can provide clarity and even solutions.

- **What are the potential consequences of standing by my values in this situation?** Weigh the outcomes of your actions, both positive and negative.
- **How can I communicate my stance effectively and respectfully?** Plan your approach to ensure your message is clear and considerate.

Upholding core values, especially as a DEI practitioner, is an ongoing process of self-awareness, courage, and persistence. It involves not only recognizing when our values are being challenged but also having the tools and strategies to address these challenges constructively. By consistently aligning our actions with our core values, we become better professionals and agents of positive change in our communities and organizations.

# CHAPTER 16
## Core Values In Action

Now that we've explored the significance of understanding personal values and living them authentically, it's time to delve into the essential process of integrating these values into your initiatives. This approach will undoubtedly strengthen your commitment and serve as a guide to setting boundaries and ensuring that your values are respected within your work. From my personal experience, I've found that aligning my personal values with my DEI initiatives not only fills my cup but also drives innovation and yields the most significant impact.

## LEAD BY EXAMPLE WITH INTEGRITY

As a practitioner, it's vital to embody the core values you're advocating for. Your personal integrity is your North Star. If authenticity is one of your core values, be true to yourself in every aspect of your work. If empathy is paramount, genuinely understand the experiences of others. Demonstrating these values not only influences your organization but also fosters personal growth and integrity.

Here are two scenarios highlighting DEI practitioners who upheld their values of honesty and respect to lead by example:

## PERSONAL SETTING: KIA, THE HONEST AND COMPASSIONATE FRIEND

Kia had always been known for her honesty. She believed in speaking the truth, but she also knew that honesty, when delivered with care, could be a powerful force for good. Among her friends, she was the one they turned to when they needed real talk—no sugar-coating, but always with respect and love.

One day, her close friend Maya was struggling. She had been stuck in the same toxic work environment for years, constantly drained and unhappy, yet unwilling to make a change. Kia had watched Maya spiral into frustration, always venting but never acting. It was hard to see someone she loved stuck in a cycle of self-doubt, and Kia knew it was time for a difficult but necessary conversation.

Over coffee one afternoon, Kia took a deep breath and said, "Maya, I love you, and I need to be honest with you. You keep saying this job is breaking you, but you're also refusing to step away. What are you afraid of? Because from where I'm sitting, staying in this place is hurting you more than leaving ever could."

Maya's eyes welled with tears, but not from anger—from relief. No one had said it to her that plainly before.

Kia reached across the table and squeezed her hand. "I'm not saying it's easy, but you deserve more than this. And I'll be here, no matter what you decide."

That moment changed things for Maya. It wasn't an overnight fix, but Kia's honesty gave her the push she needed to start looking for something better. Weeks later, Maya called Kia with excitement in her voice—she had finally put in her notice.

Kia's honesty wasn't about being blunt for the sake of it; it was about love, respect, and wanting better for the people she cared about. It was a reminder that sometimes, telling the hard truth—with kindness—is the most powerful way to show up for someone.

## PROFESSIONAL SETTING: MIKE, THE WORKPLACE AMBASSADOR FOR HONESTY AND RESPECT

Mike had always believed that honesty and respect were the foundation of a strong workplace culture. As a DEI champion in his company, he knew that fostering inclusion wasn't just about policies—it was about creating an environment where people felt safe to speak up, be heard, and be treated with dignity.

But he also knew his team had a problem. Conversations in meetings were often dominated by a few voices, leaving others hesitant to share. When disagreements arose, they turned into tense standoffs rather than productive discussions. People interrupted each other, dismissed differing perspectives, and avoided difficult but necessary conversations. Instead of collaboration, there was a quiet undercurrent of frustration.

Mike couldn't ignore it any longer. He decided to take action.

At their next team meeting, he addressed the issue head-on. "I've noticed that we're struggling to have open, respectful discussions. If we're going to work together effectively, we need to change that."

He didn't just point out the problem—he offered a solution. Mike introduced a set of *ground rules* for engagement:

- Listen to understand, not just to respond;
- No interrupting—everyone gets the space to speak;
- Disagree with ideas, not with people; and
- Assume good intent, but also acknowledge impact.

He then invited the team to share their thoughts in a structured, judgment-free way. At first there was hesitation, but as people saw that their voices were truly being heard, the atmosphere shifted. Team members started expressing concerns they had been holding back. They acknowledged past tensions and miscommunications. And for the first time in a long time, they felt like they were truly working toward solutions together.

In the weeks that followed, the changes stuck. Meetings became more balanced, discussions more open. People felt empowered to share their perspectives without fear of being dismissed. Mike's commitment to honesty and respect had set a new tone—not just for his team, but for the entire department..

In the journey of living our core values, it's essential to acknowledge that not everyone we encounter will fully understand or respect the principles we hold dear. However, our own unwavering commitment and self-affirmation are what truly matter. It's about being true to ourselves, regardless of how others respond. The responsibility of understanding and respecting our values lies with those around us, and it's their prerogative to address it.

Whether it's in personal relationships or professional settings, people like Kia and Mike exemplify the importance of staying faithful to the values of honesty and respect. Their dedication serves as a beacon of inspiration for others to follow suit. In a world where diversity, equity, and inclusion are of paramount significance, being resolute in our values is not just a personal choice—it's a catalyst for positive change in our communities, workplaces, and society as a whole. So remember, how others respond is not on you; it's on them to understand and respect the values you hold dear. Stay committed, stay affirmed, and stay true to yourself.

## INCORPORATE VALUES INTO DAILY OPERATIONS

Actively integrate your core values into your organization's daily operations. This includes everything from hiring practices to performance evaluations and project planning. Ensure that these values are not just abstract concepts but practical guidelines that shape how work is done. For instance, if transparency is important to you, consider how it can be woven into communication processes and decision-making throughout your company.

## DRIVE INNOVATION AND IMPACT

Integrating our personal values into our DEI initiatives often leads to innovation. When we approach challenges through the lens of our values, we tend to think more creatively and explore novel solutions. This innovation can have a ripple effect, positively impacting the work we do and the outcomes we achieve. It's when we bring our authentic selves to the table that the most profound changes occur.

## SHARING YOUR VALUES: A BLUEPRINT FOR SUCCESS

Sharing core values within your organization is like planting seeds of cultural transformation. Here's a detailed roadmap to help you navigate this key part of your journey:

**Craft a clear narrative:** Begin by crafting a compelling narrative around your core values. Your story should reflect not only the *what* but also your personal *why* behind these values. Then explain how they also align with the organization's mission and vision. A well-articulated narrative serves as the foundation upon which you can build understanding and enthusiasm among your colleagues.

**Engage in ongoing conversations:** Sharing values is not a one-time event; it's an ongoing dialogue. Foster a culture of continuous conversation by creating spaces for these discussions. This could include team meetings, workshops, or even informal gatherings. Encourage employees to share their thoughts and experiences related to these values. Engaging in open dialogue helps build a shared understanding.

**Lead by example:** Your actions speak volumes. Demonstrate your commitment to these values in your everyday interactions and decisions. When others see you living these values authentically, they are more likely to follow suit. For instance, if inclusivity is one of your core values, actively recruit diverse perspectives for your projects and acknowledge the contributions of all team members.

**Celebrate successes:** Recognize and celebrate individuals and teams that exemplify these values. Acknowledge their efforts and achievements publicly, reinforcing the importance of these values within the organization. And don't forget to celebrate your own! Celebrating successes boosts morale and inspires others to follow suit.

**Seek feedback and adapt:** Create channels for employees to feel safe delivering honest feedback. Encourage them to provide input on how well these values are being practiced and where improvements can be made. Use this feedback to adapt and refine your approach. Continuous improvement ensures that an organization's values evolve with its needs.

**Measure impact:** To assess the impact of sharing core values, establish key performance indicators (KPIs) related to these values. Track, measure, and share progress regularly. This data-driven approach allows you to understand how these values are influencing organizational culture and outcomes; sharing those findings creates a culture of transparency. Use the insights gained to make informed decisions and adjustments.

By following this comprehensive blueprint, you'll be well-equipped to embed core values effectively within your organization. Remember that this journey is about more than just communication; it's about fostering a culture in which these values are lived and breathed, making a lasting impact on your workplace.

## HOLDING OTHERS ACCOUNTABLE

Not everyone will share our beliefs and readily embrace the work we do. In fact, it's essential to remember that it's not our role to change people's fundamental personal beliefs around this work. Instead, the furthest we can reach is to hold them accountable for upholding their organization's expressed DEI values with the integrity and respect those commitments deserve.

Early on my journey, I realized the importance of meeting people where they are and respecting their perspectives. Fixating on those who remain resistant can be a significant distraction from the impactful work we can accomplish with those who are willing to engage. Fortunately, within any organization, there are always individuals who genuinely believe in this work, who are eager to contribute, and who are committed to this transformative journey. These are the people with whom I choose to spend my time and energy.

By concentrating on individuals who are open to change and willing to serve as role models for our values, we can create a ripple effect that inspires others to join the journey. Those who are not aligned with our values often self-select out of a culture that no longer resonates with them, and this is their personal choice.

The way I approach this work is by emphasizing that we are here to create a shared set of values and behaviors rooted in respect. When we talk about holding people accountable, it pertains to their behaviors related to work, not altering their deeply held beliefs. Beliefs are deeply personal, and we must respect individual autonomy in this regard.

Attempting to change someone's beliefs will most often be met with resistance and can lead to disappointment. Our primary goal should be to foster an environment where respect, diversity, and inclusion are practiced as shared behaviors and celebrated as shared values . We can create a workplace culture that benefits everyone, regardless of individual beliefs or backgrounds.

Now, I understand you might wonder if some individuals are just going through the motions, not genuinely committed to our cause. In such cases, the authenticity of people's engagement is not our business, nor is it where we should focus our efforts. It can be exhausting to focus on this aspect. I encourage you not to expend your energy there.

I feel strongly that our time and efforts are better spent cultivating meaningful progress rather than scrutinizing motives. If someone is engaging in the work—respecting shared values, upholding the principles of inclusion, and not causing harm—then their personal reasons for participating are not for us to police. We cannot afford to be distracted by the question of whether someone's allyship is performative if they are actively contributing to the changes we seek. Instead, let's channel our energy into building, educating, and reinforcing the expectations that shape inclusive environments. Real change requires collective action, and that action must be sustained regardless of individual motivations. If someone is showing up, aligning with the expectations we've set, and not creating harm, then they are moving in the right direction. Whether they fully believe in every aspect of the work is not for us to determine. What matters is that the work itself moves forward.

So let's stay focused on impact. Let's invest our time in those who are willing to learn, grow, and contribute. And for those whose authenticity we might question? If they are following through on what is required and honoring the shared commitment, then that is enough. The work is too urgent for us to waste time on gatekeeping sincerity.

There will always be organizational practices and policies that we may not personally agree with or find relevant. For instance, I've never been a fan of performance reviews, particularly as I have progressed in my career. I believe that my work speaks for itself, and I don't need external validation. However, if the organization has performance reviews in place, I participate because it's part of the shared group behavior, even if I personally deem it a waste of time.

It's essential to keep it real and authentic in our approach. We don't have to agree with every aspect of the organization, but as long as we're part of it, we should align with the shared values and behaviors it upholds. I want to stress that maintaining authenticity while upholding our core values and modeling this work is crucial. Sometimes, as my dear friend says, we need to "keep it 250," not just a hundred. In the end, it's not about seeking approval; it's about driving positive change within our organizations and the larger community.

# CHAPTER 17
## Measures of Success

It's important to acknowledge that success in this work isn't one-size-fits-all—it's defined differently across organizations with different business objectives. This chapter focuses on the core elements that are shared by those truly committed to diversity, equity, and inclusion and that ultimately make them successful in their missions.

While I haven't singled out specific organizations, it's not because they don't exist. In fact, despite what the media might suggest, there are many organizations deeply dedicated to this mission and doing the work required to succeed. For them, their commitment is ingrained in how they operate—it's part of their DNA. This chapter isn't about highlighting individual organizations; it's about exploring the principles and practices that guide them and showing how these values manifest in their work.

## SOCIAL NETWORK ANALYSIS

One valuable approach is to initiate a social network analysis within your organization, enabling a thorough examination of interactions among different groups and individuals. This assessment can reveal concealed patterns of inclusion or exclusion. It's imperative to identify key connectors and influencers within your network and assess their active promotion of diversity and inclusion. Armed with these insights, you can strategically devise interventions aimed at fostering cross-group connections and nurturing an inclusive culture that aligns seamlessly with your core values.

## SUPPLIER DIVERSITY SCORECARD

To expand your commitment to inclusive hiring, reaching beyond your immediate workforce and into your supply chain by implementing a supplier diversity scorecard. This method entails establishing specific objectives for collaboration with diverse suppliers, including those owned by minorities, women, and LGBTQ+ individuals. Regularly evaluate your progress in supplier diversity and transparently share these metrics with stakeholders, effectively showcasing your organization's unwavering dedication to equity across all aspects of its operations.

## CULTURAL COMPETENCY ASSESSMENTS

Another effective tool is administering cultural competency assessments to both employees and leaders. These assessments gauge awareness and understanding of diverse cultures, backgrounds, and perspectives. The results can pinpoint areas where cultural competency may be lacking and areas requiring improvement. Armed with these insights, you can tailor training sessions or workshops to address these gaps.

These unconventional measurement methods offer a distinctive lens through which to evaluate the impact of your core values on your DEI initiatives. By exploring these innovative approaches, your organization can gain a deeper understanding of its progress and, most importantly, take purposeful steps toward fostering a more inclusive and equitable workplace.

# CHAPTER 18

## The Everlasting Journey of Growth and Purpose

In the magnificent tapestry of life, our journey of self-discovery and growth is a remarkable thread. Each day offers us an opportunity to learn, evolve, and refine our values. It's a continuous process, much like the steady flow of a river that carves its path through solid rock over time. Embrace this journey with open arms, for it is the path to becoming the best version of yourself.

As you navigate the twists and turns, remember that growth often lies just beyond your comfort zone. Don't be afraid to stretch yourself, for it's in those moments of challenge that you'll find the most profound revelations about who you are and what you stand for. Your values are your compass, guiding you through the complexities of life. Stay true to them, and you'll find the strength to overcome any obstacle.

In the face of adversity, remember that setbacks are merely setups for comebacks. Every stumble is a chance to rise stronger, wiser, and more resilient than before. Your journey is a testament to your resilience and your capacity for greatness. Embrace it with a heart full of hope, for the best is yet to come.

## ENCOURAGEMENT AND EMPOWERMENT

To all you passionate practitioners of diversity, equity, and inclusion, you are the architects of change, the champions of equality, and the world's beacons of hope. Your work is not just a job; it's a calling, a purpose, a mission. Embrace the significance of your role in shaping a more inclusive world. Your efforts ripple through society, creating lasting impacts that transcend generations.

In times of doubt and uncertainty, remember the words of Nelson Mandela: "It always seems impossible until it's done." Your dedication to this cause is the driving force behind the transformation we seek. Embrace each challenge as an opportunity to demonstrate your steadfast commitment and your ability to drive real change.

Empowerment starts from within. Believe in your capabilities, your vision, and your voice. You possess the power to challenge biases, influence minds, and inspire others to join this noble journey. Your actions today lay the foundation for a better tomorrow, and your passion is the spark that ignites progress.

In the face of adversity, stand tall and resolute, for you are part of a community that stands together. Lean on each other for support, share your experiences, and celebrate your victories, no matter how small they may seem. Together, we are an unstoppable force for change, a collective voice that echoes the call for justice and equity.

In the words of Maya Angelou, "You may not control all the events that happen to you, but you can decide not to be reduced by them."

Keep your spirit unyielding, your determination unbreakable, and your heart aflame with the belief that a more inclusive world is not just possible but inevitable thanks to your unwavering commitment and tireless efforts.

*My people,*

*As we reach the culmination of this book, I want to convey my profound gratitude for your unwavering commitment to this transformative journey. Your presence within these pages is a source of immense value, and I genuinely hope that this book has offered you useful insights and meaningful reflections.*

*This work stands as a testament to our shared labor of love, where together, we have confronted the challenges, devices, and the negative rhetoric that often cloud meaningful DEI discussions. We've all heard the whispers that DEI might be faltering, and we've grappled with the perception of inadequate support. In the face of it all, please know that I see you, I comprehend the battles you face, and I am firmly by your side through every step of this journey.*

*The exercises and reflection questions woven throughout this book are the very ones that have guided and grounded me, leading me toward a fresh, invigorated sense of purpose. I share them with you because I ardently hope they offer you a clearer understanding, a renewed perspective, and a profound sense of clarity.*

*As volunteers in this noble endeavor, many of us recognize that what drives us is more than just passion—it's about living our true purpose. Each one of you deserves an environment that is safe and supportive, whether your current organization aligns with this or not. Extend grace to yourselves and* to the organization, for organizations are composed of people, and we are all individuals navigating the human experience to the best of our abilities. In challenging moments, remember the age-old adage: "Hurt people hurt people," and most of the time, it's not about us—it's about them. Don't pick it up.

It's crucial to understand that there is no quick fix in the work we do. It's an ever-evolving, continuous journey. Regardless of the labels or acronyms ascribed to it, at its core, this work is about people—their lives, their stories, and their voices. Whether or not you share my faith, I firmly believe this work is God's work, as it revolves around the well-being of people. We are here to create space for these voices to be heard.

Some of you may be well-acquainted with these sentiments, while for others they may serve as a gentle reminder to pause and reflect. Regardless, I want you to know that you possess the strength and resilience to continue. If ever you need to step away, remember that it is your right. This is your home, and you are always welcome back. Together, we will keep the torch burning, and our community will remain resolute.

DEI is not stagnant. Those with long-term experience in this field will attest to the ebbs and flows of this work. They, along with myself, will emphasize the importance of focusing on the changes we can influence and staying true to ourselves. I often remind my own leaders that I'm not a miracle worker; I work with what I have, prioritizing quality over quantity. Organizations may perpetually expect caviar on a black-eyed pea budget, but we make the most of it.

I encourage you not to be consumed by those who oppose us or act as obstacles, unless they hold the final decision-making power. They are merely distractions. Instead, let's channel our energy into sharing and nurturing the support we find within our community.

In closing, I want each of you to understand that I wholeheartedly believe in your resilience and your ability to create meaningful change. Together, we will continue this vital work, and I am profoundly honored to stand beside you on this extraordinary journey.

Thank you for being an integral part of this endeavor, and for your unwavering commitment to a more inclusive and equitable world.

With heartfelt appreciation,
Lois

## BONUS CHAPTER

# WHEN YOU'VE HAD ENOUGH: CREATING YOUR EXIT STRATEGY

There comes a moment in every DEI practitioner's journey—or in any meaningful work—when you pause to consider: *Is it time to walk away?* Whether you've grown beyond your current role, leadership has shifted priorities, or you find yourself at odds with the organization's culture, it's OK to realize and admit that you've had enough. Sometimes *you* make that choice; other times the organization decides to part ways. Whichever side initiates the exit, remember this: *You are more than your title.*

## TITLES ARE RENTED

One of the most impactful lessons I've ever received came from the leader of a financial services organization at a conference: "These titles are rented. They don't belong to us. What belongs to us is our character and how we show up" (Thasunda Brown Duckett, president and CEO, TIAA).

Roles and titles can change in an instant, but your integrity—your approach to the work and the world—and the legacy you will leave behind are yours to keep. When you realize an organization no longer aligns with your values—or if the organization decides it no longer needs your service—it's not a judgment of your worth. *It's business.* Yet because we often pour our hearts and souls into our workplaces, that business decision can feel deeply personal.

You're not wrong to feel that way. One of the hardest lessons I had to learn was that even when decisions are "just business," it doesn't erase the emotional investment we've made. But remember that the universe is still working for your good. Sometimes what feels like a loss is really an invitation to choose yourself and pursue opportunities that better honor your worth. So when you're ready to walk away, it's not quitting—it's choosing yourself. The beauty of this truth is that it reaffirms your power to protect your peace, honor your values, and continue building a legacy that's truly yours.

## LEAVING: AN ACT OF SELF-RESPECT

Leaving doesn't mean you've failed, nor does it mean you've lost your passion for the cause. In fact, choosing to walk away—especially from a toxic environment or one that isn't living up to its stated promises—can be the most powerful statement of self-respect you can make. It says, *I deserve better. I deserve to be in spaces that value my contributions and prioritize my well-being.*

Many of us have families to support, bills to pay, and futures to plan. Not everyone can afford to leave at the drop of a hat. That's where having a plan—a tangible, actionable strategy—can make all the difference. In this chapter, we'll explore how to build that plan, why it's essential to take a break between roles, and how to protect your legacy.

## HARD TRUTHS: NAVIGATING BOTH SIDES OF BEING LET GO

Sometimes, an organization shifts its focus. Maybe they've changed business priorities, or they simply don't see the value in DEI the way they once did. If you've been let go amid that change, it can feel like a gut punch. You've invested so much heart and energy into building inclusive structures, only to watch leadership decide it's no longer a top priority.

Let me be clear: This is not a reflection of your worth or the importance of the work. It's a hard truth about an organization's readiness (or lack thereof) to champion real inclusion. If you're shown the door because they've deprioritized DEI, hold onto your own moral compass—*quickly and fiercely*. Remember why you do this work in the first place. There's a community of practitioners and advocates who still value and need your voice.

Take time to reassess your goals, reaffirm your convictions, and know that your impact extends far beyond a single job. Ultimately, you're not leaving your purpose behind; you're leaving an environment that no longer aligns with it. Conversely, if you were let go because you weren't doing your job or you were causing harm, that's for you to grapple with, and I encourage you to do so with curiosity and compassion.

I've kept it real throughout this book, so let me speak plainly: I used to believe there was a special place in hell for people who hold these titles and abuse them. But over time I've learned that *hurt people hurt people*. If this is your situation—maybe you got confused about the work or let your ego overshadow the mission—I genuinely hope this lesson brings you clarity. Please take a hard, honest look at yourself—your experiences, your motivations—before you take your next step.

Whether you choose to remain in this field or decide your path lies elsewhere, I wish you well. I have a responsibility as a practitioner to say this, because I've encountered far too many self-proclaimed champions of inclusion who've caused real harm, intentionally or not. In a role as scrutinized as ours, we simply can't afford it. I said what I said, and it needed to be said.

## ACKNOWLEDGE YOUR IMPACT— AND YOUR LIMITS

It's important to recognize a painful truth: You are only as impactful as your organization allows you to be. You can fight tooth and nail, but if leadership isn't committed to meaningful change, or if priorities shift away from your work, there's only so much you can do on your own.

That's not a reflection of your value; it's a reflection of the system's capacity (or *incapacity*) for change.

To keep your perspective, take stock of your wins. Document the successes you achieved: programs launched, systems improved, people you mentored, or experiences you changed for the better. Then reflect on what's out of your control. If a system is resistant, that doesn't negate your passion or skill—it's simply the reality of an environment not ready (or willing) to evolve.

## THE FEEL-GOOD FUND (FORMERLY "F-YOU MONEY")

I used to call it "F-you money," imagining it as the ultimate financial cushion for walking away from an unhealthy environment. But over time, I realized that *anger* wasn't the emotion I wanted driving me into my next chapter. I wanted *peace*—that sense of calm and self-assuredness that comes from knowing I could leave on my own terms. So I started calling it a feel-good fund. (Note: I am not a financial advisor.)

## WHAT IS A FEEL-GOOD FUND?

- **A financial cushion:** Money set aside so you can leave a job without immediate financial panic.
- **A mental break:** Security that enables you to take a needed pause—whether that's a week, a month, or longer—before jumping into something new.
- **Emotional freedom:** Confidence that you're not leaving in desperation; you're leaving because you value yourself.

When built intentionally, your Feel-Good Fund can give you the space to heal, reflect, and decide what you truly want next—instead of rushing headlong into a new role with the baggage of the old one.

## HOW TO BUILD IT

1. **Assess financial goals:** If you share finances with a partner or spouse, schedule regular "money dates" to review your incomes, bills, and goals together. Decide how much you can each contribute and agree on the timeline for building your feel-good fund.
2. **Assign clear tasks:** Who will track expenses, who will make transfers—and schedule how often you'll check in. Transparency fosters mutual support and accountability.
3. **Examine current spending:** Keep tabs on your daily spending habits for at least one month—every receipt, grocery bill, coffee run, or subscription. Look for patterns and identify areas where you can comfortably scale back.
4. **Start small:** Once you see where your money is going, redirect any unnecessary or "nice-to-have" expenses into your feel-good fund. A small tweak—like swapping two takeout meals a week for home-cooked dinners—can free up meaningful dollars, and even 8 to 10 percent per month adds up over time.
5. **Automate your savings:** Use automatic transfers so you don't have to think about it.
6. **Consider a side project:** If possible, pick up freelance work or a small consulting gig. Diversifying your income can accelerate your savings.
7. **Seek financial advice:** If you can, talk to a financial planner or use reputable budgeting tools for a personalized strategy.

## TAKE A NECESSARY PAUSE

One of the hardest lessons I've learned is that jumping from one role to the next without a break can do more harm than good. I used to leave a job on Friday and start the next one on Monday—eager to dive into a "honeymoon phase" of new possibilities. But I never gave myself time to process the emotional baggage from my previous environment or to celebrate the things I *did* accomplish.

## DETOX FROM YOUR OLD ROLE

Give yourself space to separate from the old before jumping into the new, just like you might after any kind of breakup.

- **Feel your feelings:** Allow yourself to be disappointed, relieved, angry, or hopeful—whatever comes up.
- **Identify the lessons:** Ask yourself what skills you developed, what boundaries you should've set, and what red flags you might've missed.
- **Release old expectations:** Not every role will fulfill every hope. Let go of the idea that you "failed" if it didn't meet your vision.

## WHY THE BREAK MATTERS

Pausing between such high-intensity roles will allow you to start your new gig with intention.

- **Heal from toxicity:** Work that pushes for equity or system-wide change can be deeply personal. Give yourself time to decompress.
- **Enter with clarity:** A new role can be thrilling, but you want to start off with a clear head and an open heart free from the fatigue of your last experience.
- **Honor your well-being:** Taking a break isn't a luxury; it's a necessary part of long-term sustainability in demanding work.

## REFLECTION QUESTIONS FOR THE TRANSITION

If you can swing it—a week or two, a month, or more—use the pause to reflect on your journey and your next steps.

Here are some prompts to help guide you:

1. What feelings am I experiencing most strongly? Relief, anger, sadness, excitement?
2. Which aspects of my old role do I never want to replicate?
3. What boundaries do I need to set in my next role to protect my well-being?
4. Where do I need healing? Have I sought therapy, coaching, or advice from mentors?
5. What beliefs or mindsets am I releasing (e.g., "I have to do it all" or "I'm only valuable if I'm busy")?
6. What do I want to carry forward? Which parts of my skill set, experiences, and relationships are worth holding onto?
7. How do I define success for this next chapter in my life?

Spend time journaling, talking with trusted friends or mentors, or simply pondering these questions during a quiet walk. The goal is to move forward intentionally, rather than being swept up by the next offer just because it's new.

## YOUR LEGACY IS YOURS TO KEEP

Leaving a role—even under tense or uncertain conditions—is not an admission of defeat. It is, in many ways, a *declaration of self-respect*. You have the right to work in spaces where your values are celebrated and your well-being is prioritized. When that's no longer the case—or when you simply feel called to something else—it's OK to go. Here's how to do wo with purpose:

- **Honor your contributions:** Remember the programs, policies, relationships, and positive changes you championed.
- **Stay connected to the community:** Your purpose doesn't live in one organization. Join industry groups, mentor others, and remain active in the networks that align with your passions.
- **Remember, you are more than any title:** Your identity is not defined by a business card or email signature; it's shaped by how you show up, the impact you make, and the legacy you leave in every space you touch.

## CHOOSING YOU IS ALWAYS A GOOD OPTION

Ultimately, building your feel-good fund, taking time to pause, and investing in your own well-being are all ways to ensure that you remain in control of your career and your life. If you choose to walk away—or if an organization decides to part ways—let that be the start of a journey into spaces that reflect your true worth.

You deserve workplaces that honor your contributions, a career path that lights you up rather than burns you out, and the financial security to protect your peace at every turn. When the time comes, choose yourself and know that your legacy, your character, and your purpose are yours forever.

# APPENDIX A

# RESOURCES THAT SHAPED MY JOURNEY

These books, references, and music have fueled my growth and kept me grounded. I share them as personal recommendations—take what serves you, leave what doesn't.

**Personal Growth**

1. *The Bluest Eye*, Toni Morrison.
2. *Becoming*, Michelle Obama.
3. *Wicked: The Life and Times of the Wicked Witch of the West*, Gregory Maguire.
4. *Talking to Strangers*, Malcolm Gladwell.
5. *The Psychology of Money*, Morgan Housel.
6. *The Likeability Trap: How to Break Free and Succeed as You Are*, Alicia Menendez.
7. *Call Me Indian: from the Trauma of Residential School to Becoming the NHL's First Treaty Indigenous Player*, Fred Sasakamoose.
8. *Taming Your Gremlin: A Surprisingly Simple Method for Getting Out of Your Own Way*, Rick Carson.

**Faith and Spirituality**

1. *Holy Bible*.
2. *The Management Methods of Jesus: Ancient Wisdom for Modern Business*, Bob Briner.

3. *Let Your Life Speak: Listening for the Voice of Vocation*, Parker J. Palmer.
4. *The Purpose-Driven Life: What on Earth Am I Here For?*, Rick Warren.
5. *Emotionally Healthy Spirituality*, Peter Scazzero.
6. *Prayers from the Heart*, Richard J. Foster.
7. *The World's Religions*, Huston Smith.
8. *God Is Not One: the Eight Rival Religions That Run the World*, Stephen Prothero.

**Professional Development**

1. *Caste: the Origins of Our Discontents*, Isabel Wilkerson.
2. *Learning to Lead: the Journey to Leading Yourself, Leading Others, and Leading an Organization*, Ron Williams and Karl Weber.
3. *Multipliers: how the Best Leaders Make Everyone Smarter*, Liz Wiseman and Greg McKeown.
4. *Leaders Eat Last: why Some Teams Pull Together and Others Don't*, Simon Sinek.
5. *Inclusive Leadership: the Definitive Guide to Developing and Executing Impactful Diversity and Inclusion Strategy*, Charlotte Sweeney and Fleur Bothwick.
6. *The First 90 Days: proven Strategies for Getting Up to Speed Faster and Smarter*, Michael D. Watkins.
7. *The Visibility Mindset: how Asian American Leaders Create Opportunities and Push Past Barriers*, Bernice Chao and Jessalin Lam.
8. *Immunity to Change: how to Overcome It and Unlock the Potential in Yourself and Your Organization*, Robert Kegan and Lisa Laskow Lahey.

## The Unbreakable Playlist

Songs that held me, healed me, and helped me keep going. Scan to listen. Dance, cry, repeat.

### Theme 1: **Overcoming Adversity**

https://open.spotify.com/playlist/4hroazFGEVBE-6wiIN1tRNh?si=ODOrfJ5CQHyHian5B2K6jA

1. Beyoncé—"I Was Here."
2. DMX—"Slippin'."
3. Nas—"I Can."
4. Marvin Sapp—"Never Would Have Made It."
5. T.I.—"No Matter What."
6. Lil Wayne—"How to Love."
7. Tim McGraw—"Live Like You Were Dying."
8. Miley Cyrus—"The Climb."
9. Koryn Hawthorne—"Warriors."

### Theme 2: **Empowerment**

https://open.spotify.com/playlist/0dCl9AqMCn-f5hmLDIAJ9zw?si=tJBwN5tzSE-qbTr5k01rqg

1. Beyoncé & Jay-Z—"Boss."
2. Beyoncé—"Freedom" (feat. Kendrick Lamar).
3. India Arie—"Video."
4. Whitney Houston—"Great Love of All."
5. Anthony Hamilton—"Ain't Nobody Worryin'."
6. Kelly Clarkson—"Stronger."
7. Andra Day—"Rise Up."
8. Sia—"Unstoppable."
9. DJ Khaled—"God Did."

## Theme 3: **Faith and Spirituality**
https://open.spotify.com/playlist/1pxI6wET0RM5zN-gu4eEYd0?si=vZOEFb_bQyWdhaXWBRGB_A

1. Kirk Franklin—"I Smile."
2. Yolanda Adams—"Open My Heart."
3. The Clark Sisters—"You Brought the Sunshine."
4. Marvin Sapp—"The Best In Me."
5. DMX—"Lord Give Me a Sign."
6. Lil Wayne—"Pray to the Lord."
7. Chris Stapleton—"Broken Halos."
8. Donald Lawrence & The Tri-City Singers—"Encourage Yourself."
9. Tamela Mann—"Change Me."
10. Donald Lawrence—"Power."

## Theme 4: **Love and Relationships**
https://open.spotify.com/playlist/1pKj1E8Fae-jzDBnhd2bnIo?si=1iIITPGPSfKZPB1SgcJ4jA

1. Beyoncé—"Halo."
2. Tim McGraw—"Humble and Kind."
3. Anthony Hamilton—"Best of Me."
4. India Arie—"The Truth."
5. Chris Stapleton—"Tennessee Whiskey."
6. Extreme—"More Than Words."
7. Beyoncé and Miley Cyrus—"II Most Wanted"
8. Sugarland—"Stay."

Theme 5: **Self-Reflection and Personal Growth**
https://open.spotify.com/playlist/5j4SnZvPzP9ck1V8z18KF1?si=TqcOMkqJSwiCgiivOcHqAw

1. Nas—"Bridging the Gap."
2. Kirk Franklin—"Imagine Me."
3. India Arie—"I Am Light."
4. Koryn Hawthorne—"Speak the Name."
5. T.I.—"Live Your Life" (feat. Rihanna).
6. Lil Wayne—"Mirror" (feat. Bruno Mars).
7. Michael Jackson—"Man in the Mirror."
8. Eminem—"Lose Yourself."

Theme 6: **Social Justice and Change**
https://open.spotify.com/playlist/0Unxzx79JT7B-Z599o7WmLk?si=HKun1RN3TqKtWPyHGIVflg

1. Beyoncé—"Formation."
2. Jay-Z—"The Story of O.J."
3. Nas—"If I Ruled the World" (feat. Lauryn Hill).
4. Marvin Sapp—"Yes You Can."
5. Yolanda Adams—"Victory."
6. Chris Stapleton—"Sometimes I Cry."
7. Sam Cook—"A Change Is Gonna Come."
8. Kendrick Lamar—"Alright."

**Citations**

Amy Edmondson of Harvard Business School introduced the concept of **psychological safety** in 1999, defining it as a work environment where team members feel safe to speak up, take risks, and learn from mistakes without fear or shame. Her research showed that such environments enhance innovation, engagement, and collaboration (Edmondson, 1999).

Google's **Project Aristotle** (2012) confirmed this concept as the most critical factor in high-performing teams. Teams that embraced psychological safety outperformed others in creativity, accountability, and shared success (Google, 2015; LeaderFactor; Psychological Safety UK).

**Reference List**

- Edmondson, A. (1999). *Psychological Safety and Learning Behavior in Work Teams.* Harvard Business School.
- Google. (2015). *Project Aristotle.*
- LeaderFactor. *Summary of Psychological Safety in Teams.*
- Psychological Safety UK. *Project Aristotle Resources.*